Management Matters
By the Experts

An American Camp Association Book

Harriet Lowe, Series Editor

american
CAMP
association

enriching lives, building tomorrows

ISBN: 978-1-58518-034-9
Library of Congress Control Number: 2007920893
Cover design: Bean Creek Studio
Book layout: Bean Creek Studio
Front cover photo: Cheney Colorado Camps (Estes Park, CO)

Healthy Learning
P.O. Box 1828
Monterey, CA 93942
www.healthylearning.com

American Camp Association
5000 State Rd. 67 North
Martinsville, IN 46151
www.acacamps.org

Contributors

Andrew Ackerman is the chief operations officer of Bunk1.com. Bunk1.com provides password-protected, one-way camper email and online photo galleries. Bunk1.com also provides staffing services, custom website design, and the Bunk1.com DB online registration and camper-management system. For more information regarding this article or Bunk1.com, please contact owners@Bunk1.com or call 888-465-CAMP.

Steve Cony is a marketing consultant who assists children's camps with the development of strategic plans and the execution of marketing materials. Camp directors may contact him at 914-271-8482.

Phil DeLong is the director at Camp Gray

Bob Ditter is a licensed clinical social worker specializing in child, adolescent, and family therapy. He supervises content for Bunk1.com and can be reached via email at BobDitter1@aol.com or by fax at 617-572-3373.

Greg Friese and Associates LLC helps clients prepare for, respond to, and recover from extraordinary circumstances, emergencies, and disasters. Realistic and context-appropriate simulations, from a tabletop exercise to a full-deployment disaster exercise, prepare your organization to prevent and respond to an emergency. Contact the author via email at gfriese@charter.net or call 715-321-1800.

Minda Garr, M.S.W., has been on the faculty of the Paul Baerwald School of Social Work and Social Welfare of the Hebrew University of Jerusalem since 1981 as a lecturer in social work practice courses and academic advisor of the school. Since 1979, Garr has spent her summers at Camp Ramah in Wisconsin as camp social worker and staff trainer.

Rabbi Ronald Garr, M.A., has been on the faculty of the David Yellin Academic College of Education in Jerusalem, Israel, since 1984 as a lecturer in adult and family education. Since 1979, Rabbi Garr has spent his summers at Camp Ramah in Wisconsin as program director for 15 summers and director of staff training for 12 summers.

June Gray is one of the directors at Camp Wawenock

Beverly Hobbs, Ph.D. is currently professor and extension specialist in the department of 4-H Youth Development Education at Oregon State University. The focus of her work is the development of nonformal educational experiences that attract and engage the participation of Latino youth. As director of the Oregon 4-H Latino Outreach Project she has provided support to the Oregon 4-H Latino Olympic Summer Camp as well as to other 4-H programs that deliver education through the camp experience.

Maureen Hosty is a professor in the department of 4-H Youth Development Education at Oregon State University. She has been a 4-H Extension faculty member for 17 years both in Oregon and Virginia and has directed 4-H camps for 16 years. She provides leadership to the 4-H Wildlife Stewards statewide project currently funded by the National Science Foundation. Maureen has an M.A. degree in international development education.

David Lira Leveron has been a youth professional for the last 20 years. For the last thirteen years he has been the camp director at the Union League Boys and Girls Clubs Camp where he has succeeded considerably in increasing the number of Latino children attending summer camp. Currently, he serves on the Board of Directors for ACA, Illinois and co-chairs the Public Awareness Committee

Mario Magaña is an assistant professor and 4-H Extension faculty member for Latino Outreach at Oregon State University. He arrived in America as a migrant worker as a young man who did not speak English. Through perseverance and support, he learned English and went on to complete a bachelors degree and then a masters degree. Today he is the camp director for the successful Oregon Latino Olympic Summer Camp that reaches over 100 Latino youth each year. He also is working with Oregon Extension faculty to find new ways to reach out to Latino youth and families.

Jon Malinowski, Ph.D., is the co-author of *The Summer Camp Handbook*, a camp consultant and staff trainer, and a member of the American Camp Association's research committee.

Sandra Publicover is the manager of contracts administration at Patriot Trails Girls Scout Council.

Marge Scanlin, Ed.D., is the former executive officer, research and intellectual resources for the American Camp Association.

Missy Schenck is the co-owner of The Green River Preserve.

Ed Schirick C.P.C.U., C.I.C., C.R.M., is president of Schirick and Associates Insurance Brokers in Rock Hill, New York, where he specializes in providing risk-management advice and in arranging insurance coverage for camps. Schirick is a chartered property casualty underwriter and a certified insurance counselor. He can be reached at 845-794-3113.

Michael Shelton, M.S., C.A.C., C.E.T., is a consultant, trainer, and the director of Camp William Penn, a camp owned by the City of Philadelphia Department of Recreation. He is the author of *Coaching the Camp Coach* and *Secret Encounters: Addressing Sexual Behaviors in Group Settings*. Shelton can be reached via his website: www.meshelton.com.

Pat Smith is one of the directors at Camp Wawenock

Christopher A. Thurber, Ph.D., is a licensed clinical psychologist, camp consultant, and coauthor of *The Summer Camp Handbook*. For questions about this article suggestions for related readings or to inquire about staff training at your camp, send an email to chris@campspirit.com.

Joe Van Tassel is the assistant director at Camp Gray.

Stephen G. Wallace, M.S. Ed., has broad experience as a school psychologist and adolescent counselor. He serves as chairman and CEO of SADD, director of counseling and counselor training at the Cape Cod Sea Camps, and adjunct professor of psychology at Mount Ida College. For more information about SADD or the *Teens Today* research visit www.sadd.org.

Michael Weeks, P.E., is a professional engineer with Camp Facilities Consulting, providing specialized study, design, permitting, and construction-consultation services to the camp and conference center community. Camp personnel may contact him at 570-296-2765 or by email at campfc@ptd.net.

Daniel Zenkel is president and chief executive officer of CampGroup, LLC, which he and his father, Bruce Zenkel, founded in 1998. Prior to founding CampGroup, Dan practiced law and developed and managed real estate.

Contents

Introduction

At *Camping Magazine* it has been our pleasure over the years to introduce the camp community to a group of experts who contribute their knowledge, talent, and expertise to helping each of us address the issues that face young people, campers, staff, directors, and boards. The efforts of these capable individuals are designed to provoke thoughtful discussion surrounding the issues of the day and offer a balance of essential management and operations know-how that informs what we do and how we do it.

Whether these compilations serve as refresher courses, form the basis for staff training, fill a gap in program development, enrich an ongoing program or camp operation, or simply provide food for thought as you strive to deliver the highest quality camp experience to every individual, we believe that you will be rewarded with a renewed sense of being a part of a community that exemplifies the best in youth development practices. In every way possible, this community is firmly committed to creating summers of discovery and learning that impact every life in profound and sometimes inexplicable ways.

Part of the magic of camp is how these ideas work their way into practice and how these practices become second nature as we explore the challenges and energy that goes along with shaping the lives of the young people and staff in our charge.

To write that our contributors are the best of the best is an understatement. These articles reflect both the timeless lessons of camp and the emerging topics in the field. They are engaging, sometimes provocative, and, always, worth the price of admission.

— Harriet Lowe
Editor-in-Chief
Camping Magazine

1

How to Get the Best Price for Credit Card Processing

by Andrew Ackerman

Whatever you think you are paying for credit card processing, you are probably wrong. We will get back to this in a moment. Getting a credit card to pay camp expenses is a relatively straightforward process. Setting up your camp to access credit cards as a form of payment, is a little more complicated. To take credit-card payments in person or over the phone using a terminal, you need a merchant account. (Taking credit card transactions through your camp website is more complicated.)

When a charge is made, the money is deposited in this account, less a small fixed charge per transaction and/or a small percent of the sale. Typically, the merchant account will "sweep" the funds into your camp's checking or savings account at the end of the day. Most big banks can set up a merchant account without too much hassle.

Credit-card processors like to quote a single low rate in their ads but you actually pay that rate far less often than you think. Your merchant account statement is designed to hide surcharges and fees. Even if you checked, a particular processor's references these items are so well disguised that many happy customers are completely unaware of them.

Understanding Fees

Do not be surprised if you have to pay a one-time, setup fee. You can sometimes get this waived, especially if you are switching to a new processor and can show them a history of large payment volumes, but if this is the first time you are applying to take credit-card payments, you should expect to pay something around $100 to get started.

Note: This is a setup fee, not an application fee. You should not have to pay anything to simply apply for a merchant account.

A "statement preparation fee" is what you pay for the privilege of getting your monthly statement. Sometimes you can get this waived if you agree to receive statements exclusively via email; sometimes there is no avoiding it. If all the other costs quoted by a particular processor are reasonable, it might be worth it to accept a $5 statement-preparation fee.

Monthly Minimums

Many merchant accounts have monthly minimums. If not all the payments you have taken in a given month generate enough charges for the merchant account provider, they automatically charge you the difference. If your camp consistently receives (or expects to receive) enough payments, this may be irrelevant; however, if like most camps your revenues are seasonal, you will likely be hit with this minimum in the slow months. As a rule of thumb, multiply your total monthly credit-card revenue by the rate the credit-card processor assigns. If that number is lower than the minimum on any given month, expect this minimum fee to kick in.

Transaction Fees

Your merchant account statement includes a line that looks something like this:

AUTH COMMUNICATION FEE .... ### TRANSACTIONS AT .... .300000

What this line really means is that you are paying $0.30 for every sale, refund, and authorization that you process. If you process only a few, high value transactions each month, this $0.30 per transaction fee may not be very meaningful. If you process many, smaller transactions these fees add up. On a $10 transaction, this fee adds 3 percent to the credit card-processing costs. You will also find lines like these on your merchant account statement:

TRANSACTION CLEARED AS CORP/BUSINESS CARD...COM VI ... ###

TRANSACTION CLEARED AS WORLDCARD ...WLD MC ... ###

These are sales where the customer used a business credit card or other "rewards" type credit card (e.g., frequent flyer miles, cash back). Visa and MasterCard charge your processor 40-80 basis points (100 basis points = 1 percent) more to process these "nonqualifying" credit cards than they do for a regular "qualifying" credit card. Your processor passes these costs on to you, the merchant.

What is worse, your credit-card processor knows that you are not looking carefully at this part of your statement so they often mark these surcharges up significantly. It is unfortunately not unusual to see some of these nonqualifying credit-card surcharges run as high as 175 basis points.

Since all you are shown is the number of transaction and the total of these surcharges, it is hard for you to figure out exactly what these markups are, but you can estimate it. Your credit-card statement probably includes your average sale value (e.g., "average ticket"). At the very least, it shows you the total number of transactions ("tickets") for that month and the total dollar amount that you can divide out to calculate your average sale value. If you multiply the number of nonqualifying transactions of a certain type by your average sale value, you get an estimate of the total dollar amount of those charges. You can then divide the surcharges by that total to find out how many basis points above that "great low rate" you are actually paying on these sales. I guarantee you will be surprised.

It is not just surcharges they are adding on that are costing you. There are also savings that they are not sharing. Take a look at these two typical lines from a given day:

dd/mm/yy ... VISA SALES DISCOUNT .25000 DISC RATE TIMES .... $$$$
dd/mm/yy ... VISA DEBIT SALES DISCOUNT .25000 DISC RATE TIMES .... $$$$

Here, at least, is the rate you were promised (2.5 percent in this example). Ignore for the moment your credit-card processor's use of the word "discount" to mean the money it takes from you to process this transaction, and these lines almost make sense: multiplying your rate by the daily total dollar amount ("$$$$") yields the cost of processing those transactions (excluding the fees and surcharges we discussed earlier, of course).

"Sale" Versus "Debit Sale"

What these lines hide is the difference between a "sale" and a "debit sale." A debit sale is when the customer uses a debit instead of a credit card. Debit cards are cheaper to process by as much as 10-20 basis points, but, as mentioned earlier, many credit-card processors charge you, the merchant, the same rate and pocket the savings. What percentage of your customers use debit cards varies from camp to camp, but it is not unusual for debit cards to make up over 10 percent of the total charges. This can add up to several hundred dollars a year in additional credit card-processing costs.

Remember also that your discount rate is not set in stone. As your charge volume grows or even as you accumulate more of a credit card-processing history (and become a lower risk as far as your provider is concerned), you can get a lower discount rate, but do not expect to get it automatically. You have to ask your merchant-account provider for the lower rate. If it has been more than a year since your discount rate was set, it is time to call your provider. Do not be afraid to mention those "great low rates" you are being offered from other merchant account providers when you call.

2

Marketing—It's 51 Percent Common Sense

by Steve Cony

Some aspects of camp management are almost automatic. You need food; you call your food service. You need shirts; you email your outfitter. You have a question about risk management; you contact your insurance agent. Some tasks in camp management are less than automatic, and occasionally you feel like responding, "Listen, I'm not good at that. And, besides, I never got into the camp profession to have to do things like…"

That last sentence often ends with the dreaded M word: marketing. When it comes to marketing, there is bad news and there is good news. The bad: Everyone has her or his own definition of what marketing means, but marketing is indeed more complex than "shopping for groceries." The good news: It is not as mysterious as many think, and it often begins with simply applying common sense.

Good marketing frequently comes from people who were never formally trained as promotional professionals; and bad marketing often comes from the highest-paid corners of Madison Avenue. You can easily see examples of the latter when you turn away from a Super Bowl commercial and say "What?" That slice of bad marketing is compounded when you awake the next morning to remember the strange scenario from the commercial but have no recall of the sponsor.

Even without the benefit of an MBA, or similar preparation, you can easily conquer many marketing issues simply by stepping back, squinting at the problem, and taking the sensible approach. The best place to start is that all-important first encounter.

Common Sense Rules of Initial Contact

Operate your website like your camp.

If prospects' first exposure to your camp is your homepage, everything that happens at the moment and as a result of the next series of clicks should mirror the professionalism of your camp operation. In short, the navigability of your site represents the organization of your camp.

Be there for them.

Your website should provide all the information that is expected to be there. I recently visited the website of a large nonprofit agency that operates multiple day-camp programs. No matter where I looked, session dates and fees were nowhere to be found. Somewhat frustrated, I resigned myself to "Contact Us."

Be there when they "Contact Us."

Continuing the previous incident, I called the agency in quest of those rates and dates. The operator asked me for the age of my child. When I said "four," she transferred me to the appropriate person, but only to encounter voicemail. This was 3 p.m., in the prime of the workday, in the active camp-enrollment month of April. I hung up, and proceeded to find another camp in the area.

Answer the phone with a "camp voice."

The greeting a caller receives is often the very first person-to-person contact with your camp. If there is cheer and exuberance, you are indeed a camp worth getting to know. After all, you have begun to fulfill the person's perceptions of camp as a fun place. If, however, the caller hears a sort of downbeat or perhaps even sullen voice, it will be that much harder to overcome a negative first impression. Anyone who doesn't have a real "camp voice" must let the phone ring and wait for voicemail to do the job. Better yet, because voicemail is always a disappointment to the caller, train those who tend the phone.

Record your voicemail message with a "camp voice."

Use your URL as your email address. Nothing makes you look more like an amateur than continuing to use addresses such as AOL, Comcast, Hotmail, etc. These are great email services for interpersonal communications, but you must look like "a player" if you are to be taken seriously. You must be xxxx@name-of-camp.com

By now, you may have realized that no advanced degree in marketing is necessary to reach these kinds of conclusions. What does form a solid foundation for good marketing decision-making is simply to take a moment, figuratively stand back, and think about the marketing issue at hand with the good sense and logic you possess. How many times is a first-time caller greeted by a rushed or even gruff or perhaps surly voice in the camp office? How often does a Web surfer become frustrated with the navigation on a camp website and immediately defect for another option?

Recognizing the importance of easy navigation, friendly phone contact, and an email address that makes you and your camp look established are all conclusions based on common sense, no MBA required.

Common Sense Rules of Message Creation

Perform a brand identity alignment.

You have never seen the golden arches rendered in green, nor have you seen the name Coca-Cola® rendered in an Old English font. Yet many camps choose a font and a visual setting for their name (a logo), then proceed to type that name in a variety of fonts and styles. You might even call it "font du jour," relying on whatever happens to be in use by the word processor when the next bulletin or fact sheet needs a header. The result is an easily detectable lack of consistency, and this translates into perceptions of carelessness. To some parents, careless camps lose campers in the woods.

Make your accreditation credible.

You worked hard to earn your ACA accreditation, yet that important symbol communicates very little on your website or brochure unless parents understand its significance. Until our accreditation is as universally understood, as is the *Good Housekeeping* seal of approval, you need to explain its importance, in terms of meeting and exceeding a comprehensive collection of standards. It's a sales-inducing story; somebody has to tell it; and that somebody is every single accredited camp.

Don't deliver everyone else's message.

If everyone is saying the same thing, and a family is reviewing these similar or near-identical messages, the end result for your prospects is confusion. If, however, you choose to deliver the different message, or even just the uniquely stated version of what everyone else is saying, you stand a much better chance of careful consideration. Some examples of same-old-same-old: lifelong memories, counselor-to-camper ratios, number of nurses on site, and "the best possible camp experience anywhere."

Cancel the helicopter and stop panning pine trees.

Aerial photography is wasteful, if you agree with that last rule about not delivering everyone else's message. From the air, your pine trees, waterfront, baseball diamonds, and buildings look like those of all other camps. This message goes for many more photos that are indistinguishable from many others when brochures are laid edge to edge on a coffee table, and that's what happens during the decision period.

Don't be cute.

Although parents do like to view photos of cute kids, it is only common sense that they prefer to see their cute kids. If you use all the photo "real estate" in your brochure or on your website for shots of campers just mugging at the camera in "say cheese" poses, you bypass the opportunity to show what really happens at camp. Parents and children are much more interested in seeing what campers actually do at camp—the activities.

Tidy up your print materials.

If your envelope is filled with bulletins, calendars, enrollment forms, health forms, and more that all look like they have been run over and smudged by a truck, you will create an instant impression of disorganization and amateurism. Today it is no longer acceptable for anyone, even a very traditional summer camp, to appear "back-woods," because consumers understand how easy it is for everyone to look consistent and professional.

Be perfect.

Camps often go to great lengths to boast that most of the staff are educators during the school year. Then some of those same camps produce marketing messages with poor grammar, usage, punctuation, capitalization, and misspelled words. Common sense says that this is not evidence of the work of educators. Though camp may be back-to-basics to some, and even "laidback" to others, the summer lifestyle does not permit typographical chaos. It is worthwhile to have your materials proofread by professionals once the writing is complete, and this service is easily and economically available online.

Prove that you're in a kid business.

Camps tell parents that everything done is ultimately for the safety, fun, and development of the camper. Yet how many marketing campaigns address the child directly? If a child is part of the decision process, and we know that children's role in choosing is steadily growing, then should we not be communicating with them? Not blatant selling in their faces, but letting them perceive that we know they are out there. Even if the child in a family does not pour over our special message to him, the parent sees that we have put our money where our mouth is about being child-centered.

Common Sense Rules of Message Delivery

Get in their face.

Just like you see most products' TV commercials multiple times, your message needs to be seen more than once. That means more than a single, isolated advertisement, and it certainly calls for assertive follow-up after a family makes an initial contact. Once an interested party receives your brochure and perhaps a video, a next mail piece should talk about FAQ's and selling points worthy of repetition.

Capture the data.

Make sure to record complete contact information from every prospect. Then build a database for future mailings and emailings. When people ultimately turn you down, find out why. You will learn more from these rejecters than might be gained from talking to loyal supporters.

Keep the site in sight.

Set aside time one day per month to visit your own website, confirm that everything is working, and update any outdated information. Never use the words 'Under Construction' anywhere on your site; if something is not ready, remove the button.

Stay the course.

Too often camp directors press the marketing accelerator when enrollments slip a bit, but coast along when they are sold out or nearly so. Because marketing is built on achieving a permanent position in people's minds, it is a task that must be continuous. You have no control over when prospects begin thinking about camp, so you must be there at any conceivable time that their process begins.

The Other 49 Percent

Having presented the case for common sense as 51 percent of marketing, here are a few words about the other 49 percent: Common sense is the first step toward sound marketing strategy. However, strategy is not simply the application of common sense. It is an orderly process of thinking about your market, your target audience, and your competition. It is not something that just happens by itself as you publish the annual details of each camp season. Rather, it is the determination of your "big story"—what makes your camp experience different and better, for the camper and for the family.

Remember that rule cited above, the one about not delivering everyone else's message? The strategic development of your marketing message will help you to prevent this all-too-prevalent me-too-ism.

The rest of the remaining 49 percent of the equation leads to the need for creativity. Too often camp professionals look at other advertising in the marketplace and respond, "Too cute. Too hokey. Too commercial. Definitely not camp-like." However, it becomes more evident every year that camp is being purchased like many other products and services. In the 21st century, purchasers expect to be "sold" the things that they will buy. They want to be marketed to. In our increasingly commercial marketplace, fewer and fewer products and services retain a special status where consumers excuse them from competing.

Perhaps there was a time when all camp had to do was publish the annual rates and dates, and the enrollment floodgates would open. In some communities and/or for some individual camps, that situation might still exist. For most, however, you need to assertively vie for attention, interest, desire, and action on the part of the purchasing family.

The first step is attention. There is no better way to turn someone's head in your direction than to do something creative. For example, consider a simple print advertisement. A crisp layout can help your message to outperform the other same-old-same-old messages on the page.

The headline shares the job of attracting attention with the layout, and then it goes on to create interest. The name of your camp is not a headline, and should not appear as the most prominent words in the space. Instead, a short and intriguing sentence functions to draw the reader in. The name of your camp belongs somewhere at the bottom. The same rule applies to your website homepage and the cover of your brochure. Translated to video, this makes a good case for showing something surprisingly different in the very first scene.

Once you gain attention and take prospects to the next step of interest, it is time to create desire. This is where you match the camp experience you offer with the needs of your target audience. What do you do differently and better than other camps being considered? More important, is this perceivable difference something that your market values?

To turn desire into action, offer reasons to act now. Announcement of rapidly mounting enrollments, early bird discounts, and special incentives put urgency into the selling process.

Your prospects approach you asking, "Why should I choose you?" If you do not attempt to successfully answer that question, be prepared to lose to your competitors. While common sense can drive many marketing decisions successfully, there is no substitute for inspired creativity to attract the attention you deserve for the camp experience you create every summer.

3

A Time for Reflection

by Bob Ditter

Taking Stock

Here in New England the late summer days of September and early October comprise a season unto themselves. Cooler at night, with warm, dry days, earlier evenings and the bounty of the harvest at its peak, it is a time for renewal and reflection. Late summer is a slower time for most camp professionals, even those with a thriving shoulder season, as the engagement with post-camp groups seldom matches the intensity of camp sessions. Like educators, for camp professionals September is often the start of a new year. Unlike educators, however, who have new classes and students to contend with, it is a perfect period for reflection, with an eye toward carrying forward the best of the just-completed season.

Camper-Counselor Success Stories

One practice I strongly recommend is taking the time to record specific examples of breakthroughs or positive experiences that campers had this summer while they are still fresh in your mind. Like the 13-year old boy Jake,* diagnosed with ADHD, who had a terrible experience the year before at another camp, but this year, his first at your camp, made two solid friends and had the summer of his life because of the careful preparation you and your staff did before he arrived.

---

*Author's note: Examples are composites of actual situations I have encountered at camps across the United States and are used for illustrative purposes. Names of campers have been invented to protect their privacy.

Were you to write down the details of this situation, you would be sure to note how you had a trusted returning staff member call Jake before camp; how that counselor found out what Jake's interests were and connected him to a few of the other returning campers in his group via the Internet (so they could, with their parents' permission, share their interests and stories about camp by email); and how you had the boys' head counselor in Jake's unit speak with his parents and his therapist to gain insight about what strategies might best work with Jake if his ADHD started to get the best of him at camp.

Then there is nine-year old, Sara, whose mother had given birth to a new baby just before Sara came to camp. Terribly homesick for six days straight, one of your innovative female counselors, with your permission, had Sara's mother email the camp some pictures of the baby, which Sara's counselor gave her to use as part of a "girls' circle show-and-tell" sharing during rest hour. Under the guiding hand of the counselor, the sharing circle grew into a sharing time for all the girls, in turn strengthening the bonds among them, which not only helped abate Sara's homesickness, but also increased their feelings of friendship.

At the end of the session, the girls created a booklet, which they each got a copy of, with all the things they had shared as a way to mark their friendship and their time at camp. There were stories and poems and drawings and other mementos the girls had included that became their own group "camp yearbook."

Great Counselor Initiatives

You might also record things your counselors did during the summer that you want to be sure to share with your staff next summer as an example of the fine practices you hope to see in all your staff. Too often camp directors share only the negative behaviors or mistakes of counselors, giving staff an earful of frustrated and fretful examples of poor counselor performance.

What every crop of new staff can use are clear, specific examples not only of the breakthroughs campers have had, as suggested above, but also the sincere efforts of their predecessors, such as the male counselor who practiced what I call "building momentum" as a way of getting his 12-year old reluctant campers out of bed every morning. First getting himself and his co-counselor up and dressed just before reveille, they put on music and got the less resistant campers out of bed first thus creating "momentum" that carried over to the more retiring members of their group.

The day camp group leader who, in an effort to keep a wandering camper with the group, allowed him to carry her clipboard and whistle and lead the other campers from one activity area to the next at transition time. When other campers protested that they, too, would like a turn at this honorable role, the quick-thinking counselor gave her meandering camper the job of selecting who should take his place, thus retaining for him a different special role as a reward for staying with the group.

Best Performers

Another important note to make before too much time has elapsed is a list of your best staff performers from this season. Consider having them think about friends from back home or at their college or university who they think would fit well into your camp and be strong additions to the staff next year. Experience shows that staff that are strong, performers and feel valued by a camp, especially if they themselves came initially as outsiders and developed a fondness or strong positive connection to the camp, will only refer friends whose personalities and work ethic they think would complement the values and principles of that camp.

Given their newly established high positive regard for camp, they take a personal stake in which of their friends would also be effective performers. Anything less would be a bad reflection on them. Through this "filter of concern," new members referred by current staff often have a work ethic and level of commitment similar to their friends.

I know of one camp in Pennsylvania that several years ago had one counselor from Nova Scotia who proved to be an exceptionally fine member of the staff. He was asked to refer friends from home who would enjoy the camp, fit in, and be good workers. Because this counselor had developed a warm, positive feeling for the camp, he took this request seriously and only referred people he thought would be successful there. Even though he was given a bonus for each staff member that was hired, a factor some camp directors would consider a conflict, the people he referred have consistently been great performers. Today that camp has a significant number of staff members from Nova Scotia who consistently perform at a high level and add spirit and character to the camp.

Refining Your Camp's Mission

Late last May I heard the startling fact that over 6,000 children in the United States had been expelled from preschool. Were preschool children really so wild or was there another explanation, I wondered? What I subsequently learned was that preschool, once a place for children to learn how to play, get along with one another, and become accustomed to being away from their primary caretakers for several hours at a time, were now required to learn the alphabet, count, know their colors, and be able to spell their name. It would seem that play has been abandoned for early academics.

Camp professionals know that play is more than just fun; it is a medium for helping children develop coping skills. It is through play that campers learn to wait their turn, ask for help, accept instruction, support others, manage and get beyond their fears and apprehensions, recover from setbacks, tolerate frustration, and experience mastery and success.

In other words, play is how children learn to cope, to know they are more than what they happen to be feeling in a given moment, and to become more civilized and resilient. Knowing how to count to 20 and spell your name before kindergarten, while useful, does not build these coping skills.

Interestingly enough, 6,000 preschool children have already told us they would rather not be in a place where play and all its lessons are not offered. Why else would they kick up such a stink so as to get thrown out? A well-devised, well-guided camp program teaches, in a fun and memorable way, coping and resilience. Rest up, camp folks, because there is obviously still a lot of work to be done.

4

Changing Practices to Meet a Growing Concern

by Bob Ditter

The verbal and physical abuse and intimidation of campers by other campers has been receiving increasing attention from both parents and camp professionals alike. In a 1999 survey of several insurance companies that count camps among their clients, I found that up to 24 percent of "crisis calls" to the hotlines of those companies involved incidents of camper-to-camper abuse; at the time, this was second only to calls about inappropriate, intimate behavior between counselors and campers. More recently, concerns about teasing and bullying spawned a front-page article in *The New York Times* ("Hot Topic at Summer Camps: Ending the Rule of the Bullies," June 28, 2004). The concern about potential bullying behavior at camp is growing.

The apprehension of parents has been easy to track and has increased perceptively since September 11. Combined with violence in schools a la Columbine, the Catholic priest child-abuse scandal (which is viewed by most people as a crisis in trust and not just a "Catholic" problem), hair-raising stories about initiations and hazing events among high school sports teams, and the worry over terrorism, parents have a more generalized anxiety about the safety of their children and the credibility of those charged with their care and well-being. The movie *Mean Girls* has been widely viewed by parents and offers clear examples of just the kinds of situations they don't want their children to face.

Training staff to look for signs of mistreatment of campers by other campers and to intercede in firm, yet respectful ways (bullies need guidance, too) is clearly important in addressing the problem, and from the anecdotal evidence presented in the June 28 *Times* article, more and more camps are including some sessions on bullying and teasing in their orientation. This is a laudable trend, which I hope continues. However, staff training alone is not enough to corral the problem of bullying. Like the challenge of inappropriate behavior of campers by staff, there must be improved supervision of campers in order to effectively reduce the incidence of cruel behavior of campers by other campers.

Most people experienced in the care and supervision of children know that teasing and bullying can be extremely subtle and persistent. Mean looks when adults are momentarily distracted, a whispered threat, a clandestine note, or being quietly ostracized and shunned by peers are all refined forms of systematic abuse. I recall visiting an eight-week coed resident camp in Pennsylvania just a few years ago where several girls had been terrorized by the rest of the group right under the noses of their counselors. The problem came out in the open when, during parent visiting day, the girls spilled their tearful stories to their parents. In addition to the subtle nature bullying can have, many counselors become either tired or so acclimated to the teasing, children often engage in that they cannot judge what is "normal give-and take" and what may constitute abusive behavior.

Regular Staff Check-Ins

The need for better supervision of campers, starting with better check-ins with bunk staff, has become increasingly important. As it stands now at most camps, sometime during orientation a member of the administration tells staff that "we are here for you," exhorting staff to seek out help when confronting challenging camper behavior. While this is a good practice and should be continued, it largely doesn't work. Most staff are too worried about how they will be perceived or what the administration might think were they to seek out such help. In addition, many staff assume they should know how to deal with the challenges of campers and often won't allow themselves to admit when they are in over their heads. They often worry that a unit director or head counselor will step in and take the problem out of their hands, essentially undermining their authority or credibility with campers. To overcome these roadblocks, formalized check-ins with staff should be instituted as a regular part of the program at camp. I myself engaged in this practice when I was involved with America's Camp, the one-week session held at Camp Mah-Kee-Nac in August for children who had family members who perished in the 9-11 attacks.

Sitting with the staff of individual bunks for thirty minutes each day brought to light numerous behaviors that might otherwise have remained unknown to the administration. Many of these challenging behaviors were well handled by the superb, handpicked staff at America's camp, but the experience convinced me that regular check-ins can be a helpful part of a "check-and-balance" system of supervision at camp.

I suggest setting up a list of "check-in questions" to be given to all staff near the end of orientation with an explanation of how the check-in works along with the schedule of meetings. (For most camps, once or twice a week would be practical and effective.) This way your bunk staff can prepare and will understand your expectations. The following is an example of such a list:

Tell me about any camper who…

- is having a persistent problem with homesickness.
- seems to be separating herself from the rest of the group.
- doesn't seem to have or be making friends.
- is dominating or manipulating the group.
- doesn't seem to be eating.
- has a problem with personal hygiene.
- has had a bed-wetting accident.
- has had a nightmare or sleep disturbance.
- has been in a fight.
- has been having temper outbursts.
- has shared something upsetting with you or other campers.
- is overly preoccupied with sexual matters.
- has been asking overly personal or sexual questions of you or other counselors.
- has displayed some kind of inappropriate sexual behavior (name-calling, storytelling, graphic language, simulating sex).
- has been sick or gotten hurt.
- has bruises, a rash, or other sign of a physical problem.
- has refused to go to activities.
- has been found with contraband in the cabin, bunk, or tent (including medication).
- has been threatening to run away.

The above list can easily be modified for day camps.

Checking With Staff About Staff

Along with a thorough list of check-in questions regarding campers, include questions about fellow staff that provide additional confirmation, as follows:

Tell me about any adult…

- whose behavior with campers is making you uncomfortable, such as being threatening or punitive with campers.

- using inappropriate language or gestures with campers, touching campers in a way that doesn't seem right.

- doing or saying something inappropriate in front of campers.

- whose behavior with another counselor is making you uncomfortable (e.g., threatening or harassing someone, including in a sexual way or using inappropriate language or gestures).

- touching someone in a way that doesn't seem right.

- who you feel is stressed or who you think could use some support or relief.

- who you feel is not taking care of him or herself.

- who may be keeping medications or other contraband in the bunk.

The Evening Watch

Many resident camps have long had a practice of allowing staff to leave for the evening, keeping a smaller crew behind to keep watch over multiple cabins, tents, or bunks. Given that much intimidation and abuse occurs after "lights out," when adult supervision is at its lowest level, this practice is simply not in keeping with the goal of providing an emotionally and physically safe environment for children. How many times have I seen parents become uneasy when they learn that an adult is not always physically in the bunk at night with campers. If camp professionals are serious about maintaining the safest surroundings for campers humanly possible, then the number of adults present with campers at night must be reviewed. Though not a popular move, it is one of the weakest areas of supervision in resident camps today.

Meeting the Challenge

Most camps have activities that involve risk, like horseback riding, archery, high ropes-course elements, climbing towers, etc. Even having a waterfront is a risk. Yet, through careful training and the application of particular protocols, camps have consistently been able to run these activities at a high level while reassuring parents and keeping campers safe. It is time to apply this same expertise to the realm of supervision, since it may turn out that the riskiest activity is simply having campers in the company of other campers. Camps can meet that challenge.

5

Emergency-Response Drills for Camps

by Greg Friese

Fortunately, many of our camps will never experience a true emergency—serious accident or fatality, financial collapse, program crippling property damage, or mission threatening negative publicity. A clean record does not guarantee a smooth future. Recent events like multiple swimmers drowning, abuse allegations, vehicle accidents, and wildfires remind us of the importance of having an emergency-response plan. The best way to test your plan and crisis team is to conduct an emergency-response drill.

Types of Drills

Emergency-response drills are categorized by complexity. Drill types include a plan walk-through, tabletop exercise, event simulation, or full-deployment drill (Kamer, 2003). As complexity increases the drill length, stress on participants, necessary resources, and duration increase. Pick a drill type based on organization knowledge, experience, and resources.

Plan Walk-Through

A plan walk-through introduces the crisis team to the emergency-response plan. In a staff meeting, review key points of the plan, when it is implemented, and how it is executed. Refer participants to communication pathways, guidelines for speaking to the media, emergency-contact phone lists, and emergency procedures. Conduct a plan walk-through when a new program is initiated, like a challenge course, or as a new full-time staff member is hired. It is a great chance to review roles and responsibilities by discussing what-if scenarios, like a fall at a climbing site or a whitewater kayaking drowning. A plan walk-through sparks discussion on preventing and responding to those horrible "what ifs."

Tabletop Exercise

During a tabletop exercise, crisis-team members respond to incoming information about a hypothetical crisis as if it were real. A moderator and role players feed crisis-team members details as the scenario unfolds. For example, a scripted role player calls the program office, "This is a drill. This is Sgt. Friday, reporting a camp van rollover on highway 15 with multiple injuries." During the drill, the crisis-team leader assigns tasks and facilitates resolution of the crisis.

A tabletop is a communication exercise and can have varying degrees of intensity and duration depending on the organization's needs. Allow several hours for execution and debriefing improvements to the plan and assessing team function.

Event Simulations

Event simulations increase the level of realism and intensity. For example, Wilderness Medical Associates wilderness first-responder students respond to simulated accident scenes, complete with fake blood and screaming patients with simulated injuries. Students know it is a drill, but the level of stress is palpable and helps prepare them for a real medical emergency. As the realism increases, it is critical to have observers to ensure safety, evaluate individual and team performance, and prepare feedback for participants. In likely outdoor-program emergencies, the response and patient-care phases are usually low duration. Consider extending the event simulation to include evacuation to safety, communication to external audiences, and program continuity considerations. An event simulation could last two to eight hours or longer. Like a real incident, encourage participants to rest and recover afterwards. Conduct your evaluation the next day after everyone is comfortable, relaxed, and fed.

Full-Deployment Drill

A full-deployment drill is as real as possible. They are typically used in law enforcement, aviation, or health-care settings to prepare for situations like bioterrorism, plane crashes, or hostage rescue where the incident could last for days. The duration simulates the fatigue, staff changes, and planning cycles that occur in a long incident (Kamer, 2003).

A full-deployment drill requires extensive planning and a major commitment of time and resources. It is unlikely a camp would independently respond to a full-scale disaster. More realistically, you would be one of many affected by a hurricane, wildfire, or bioterrorism incident. Contact your local Red Cross, emergency-management officials, law-enforcement agencies, or health-care providers to participate in a regional emergency prevention and response program. Maybe your facility could become a treatment area or evacuation site during a natural disaster, like the 2003 California wildfires.

Conducting an Emergency-Response Drill

To start planning, ask yourself, "What is our worst-case scenario?" Script how that situation could unfold, identify parties involved, and set goals for the drill. Phases of conducting a drill include:

- An emergency-response plan needs to be in place and supported by administration.
- The crisis team is aware of roles by doing a plan walk-through and is committed to drill goals.
- Prepare role players. Script the time of their interaction, lines, questions, and emotions. Realism increases learning.
- Brief the crisis team on necessary background information and how the drill will unfold. Emphasize imagination, effort, and participation.
- Conduct the drill. Follow a script for delivering information and assigning tasks to the crisis team. Observe the crisis team.
- Debrief the drill. Identify positive team and individual actions, flaws in the plan, and areas for improvement.
- Celebrate.

Emergency-response drills are an excellent way to improve emergency planning and communication. If you do not have an emergency-response plan, you need one. Test the plan every year. Conduct a plan walk-through when new administrative staff are hired or for major program changes. An annual tabletop exercise keeps your plan relevant and the team sharp. Unlike a real emergency, drills can be fun, but they are also stressful. Reward your team with a meal or social opportunity afterwards. Practice for the thing that keeps you awake at night and you may start to sleep better.

References

Ajango, D. Editor. (2000). *Lessons Learned, A Guide to Accident Prevention and Crisis Response.* Alaska Outdoor and Experiential Education.

Herman, M. L. and Oliver, B. B. (2001). *Vital Signs: Anticipating, Preventing, and Surviving a Crisis in a Nonprofit Risk Management Center.*

Kamer, L. (2003). *Preparing and Fine-Tuning your Crisis Plan: A Workable Methodology.* Larry Kamer. Kamer Consulting Group. www.bizforum.org/whitepapers/kamer.htm.

6

Establishing Clear Limits

by Rabbi Ronald Garr, M.A. and Minda G. Garr, M.S.W.

One of the major challenges of working with a pre-adolescent and adolescent camper population is the area of boundary setting and limits. David Elkind (1994) describes the major psychological issue of middle to late childhood (6-11) as the conflict between the desire to grow up and enjoy the benefits of adulthood versus the desire to remain a child, enjoying the accompanying benefits. In Erikson's (1950) model of psychosocial development, adolescence (12-18) is the fifth stage, with the main conflict to be resolved that of identity versus role confusion, and the development of peer relations as one of the major events of this age group. Elkind (1994) speaks of the importance of establishing a stable and resilient sense of identity. Adolescents need to make sense of their experiences and to learn about themselves.

These are the children that make up our camper population. They come to camp to learn about themselves and to make sense of their interactions with others. They come to a safe environment where they can try on new and different behaviors that might not be acceptable at home. They come to a place where they can try on new roles and new experiences, trying to unravel the mystery of the transition from childhood to adolescence and the next transition from adolescence to adulthood.

One of the pivotal elements in structuring a successful camp experience for campers is the establishment of clear limits and expectations. Counselors are often surprised when confronted with camper behaviors that are difficult to manage in the cabin or in the activity area. Not recalling their own experiences as campers struggling with the many conflicts and issues of childhood and adolescence, counselors often believe that trust and kindness are sufficient conditions for a warm, cooperative atmosphere in the cabin setting. They sometimes feel angry and hurt when treated disrespectfully by their campers who seem unable to live and work harmoniously together. They may feel resentful and exploited.

What is the Source of This Problem?

Most children who come to camp want to have a positive experience. They want to feel loved, encouraged, protected, and safe. However, what is easy to forget is that they are still children, and their expressed reasons for coming to camp are to be with their friends and to have fun. In addition, for some campers, some of the time, having fun means being able to do whatever they want, whenever they want, with no limits. For camp staff and educators, finding ways to balance campers' need for fun, and adult understanding of the importance of behavior management and limit setting represents a major challenge.

Young campers may have difficulty controlling their behavior in a group setting and may be too young to take on this responsibility. The freedom of being far away from home and school and living in a cabin with others their own age is a stimulating and exciting experience. There are many times when they need an external structure and our active support to behave in ways that are not only fun, but also inclusive of others. They need to be guided by a sense of mutuality, respect, and direction.

Older campers may also engage in disruptive behavior, but the motives are different. As they make their way from childhood to adulthood, no longer children but not yet adults, they are struggling to figure out who they want to be and who they are. One of the ways this struggle is expressed in the camp setting is in their interactions with authority figures—cabin counselors, activity counselors, unit heads, and teachers. They confuse the staff and themselves as they waver between resenting adult authority; feeling they should be treated as "equals"; and indicating in sometimes subtle ways that they should be able to count on the "adults" for support, guidance, and protection. These conflicting feelings can lead to puzzling and sometimes inappropriate behaviors, as they vacillate between wanting to be treated as equals and yet to be guided and protected. Eventually problems may develop in the camper-staff relationship.

The Struggle

The struggle witnessed in the camp setting is an external projection of the turbulence within as these adolescents struggle to grow into adulthood. Adolescent campers may at times be defiant, rigid, arrogant, and egocentric. At other times, they will be caring, sensitive, attentive, and thoughtful. Adolescent campers often are not "pliable." They expect to hear "reasonable" explanations to all requests and demands, but "reasonable" often has to follow their logic. The life of the counselor may be difficult, but it is never boring.

When functioning as a group, there are some additional reasons that may contribute to disruptive behaviors. One of the first things campers need and want to know when they begin the summer in a new cabin group is the limits of acceptable behavior. Asking what the rules are is one way to discover what these limits are. However, one of the important facts of the informal communication network in camp is that some rules are not as important as others, and only some rules will really be enforced. Campers will "test" the rules to discover which ones the staff is really committed to enforcing. "Testing" implies experimenting with behaviors that disrupt the prescribed or expected framework of cabin behaviors and/or camp activities, and to see what, if anything, will be the response. This testing period may vary, depending on the willingness and ability of the staff to establish boundaries and to clearly and firmly enforce a framework of acceptable behavior early in the camp season.

There is also a camp-specific reason why campers engage in unacceptable behavior. The "testing period" is likely to be more pronounced in the camp setting than it might be in noncamp settings. The informal setting and the more complex relationships that the campers have with the counselor as compared to a teacher at school, can contribute to a lack of clear hierarchical boundaries. This lack of clarity has an impact on counselors as well as campers. It is the responsibility of the counselor through words and action to define this ambiguous and sometimes confusing relationship.

It is the job of the counselor to convey to campers that in spite of relaxed dress and setting, and in spite of first names and multi-faceted relationships between counselor and campers, they have a clear mutual goal on which to focus—building a well-functioning group unit that knows how to play together, work together, and be together, in a framework of cooperation, mutual respect, and consideration. This goal is not conveyed when a counselor is absent from the cabin at critical times during the day and evening, routinely begins activities late, is unprepared, or does not insist on cabin and activity behaviors that contribute to growth and learning.

Peer influences are more prominent in a camp setting. Parents are far away, most daily interactions are with others of the same age, and counselors are sometimes only a few years older than they are. When a popular child chooses the path of misbehavior, others may follow unless there is a clear adult presence that can help campers look at the consequences of their actions.

Another reason why children who do well in school and other social settings may choose inappropriate behaviors in camp is based on an often healthy need—the need to experiment with new roles and behavioral options. They are far away from the immediate influence of their families, schools, and friends at home. With none of the usual constraints in place, campers have the opportunity to experiment. They try out new ways of presenting themselves to others and of interacting with adults and peers.

At home, they may be afraid or locked into habitual roles and behavioral patterns, but at camp they may be able to try something new and different.

This is one of the great opportunities of camp life. Children trust that they are in a protected environment, one in which it is safe to experiment without worrying about parental reactions. For example, the child who is almost too "good" at home may experiment with acting out at camp, looking for ways to be noticed by "talking back" or "getting in trouble." It is important for the camp staff to support the efforts of children to experiment with new roles, but at the same time to insist that this experimentation take place within reasonable limits that do not undermine the basics of emotional health and safety within the camp community.

The Challenges

Serious challenges to senior staff arise as junior staff members sometimes seem hesitant to identify, notify, and enforce even the minimal rules in a serious way. There are several reasons for this. Often, cabin counselors are initially very uncomfortable being in positions of authority and managing the behavior of campers. They may wonder if they have the right to tell campers what they can and cannot do. They may fear that if they set limits, campers will dislike them. As a result, new and even veteran staff members may try to completely circumvent the problem of a hierarchy and authority. They will present themselves to the campers as friends or as equals and directly or indirectly try to make a deal with the campers:

- "We will be nice to you, if you will be nice to us."
- "We don't want to be mean counselors who are constantly saying, 'Stop this! Do that!'"
- "We don't want to be your enemies. Since friends respect each other, let's just get along…"

This approach is rarely successful. Very quickly, the counselor is likely to find campers are taking full advantage of his trusting attitude. Almost before the counselor realizes it has happened, the cabin or activity group is out of control, and the counselor is feeling personally insulted, demoralized, and very angry with the campers. At this point, the counselor may try to change his approach, trying to establish himself in the role of authority he had previously rejected. In his attempt to do something different, he often becomes overly strict.

Campers are confused as the counselor moves from a laid-back approach to behavior management to a strict authoritarian approach. They've gotten used to the counselor as their pal, and at this point it is very difficult to make a change. The counselor is feeling mad and frustrated with the campers, experiencing the group as out of control, and campers are angry and upset because the counselor is changing both the rules and his own behavior.

Staff Training

Although possible, it is challenging to make a successful change mid-session in management style. We suggest that it is more effective for counselors to explore some of the issues relating to limit setting, boundaries, and the use of authority before the camp season begins.

Knowing what to expect can be helpful in handling behaviors that are disruptive, or hopefully even preventing situations that may lead to hurt and angry feelings on both sides. A firm and clear approach to behavior management can make the difference between an exciting and meaningful summer experience and a confused and chaotic experience. Being clear does not mean being mean. Being firm does not mean being distant and uncaring. Children know we care about them when we provide an environment that is structured, with lots of room for play; an environment that has limits, with lots of room for caring and support; and an environment with clear boundaries where they can know for sure they are safe and protected.

References

Dinkmeyer, D. (1998) *Parenting Teenagers: Systematic Training for Effective Parenting of Teens (STEP)*. Circle Pines, American Guidance Service.

Elkind, D. (1994). *A Sympathetic Understanding of the Child*. Boston: Allyn and Bacon.

Erikson, E. (1950). *Childhood and Society*. New York: Norton.

Mackenzie, R. (1997) "Setting Limits in the Classroom." *American Educator* 21, Fall. 32 - 43.

Steere, B. (1968). *Becoming an Effective Classroom Manager: A Resource for Teachers*. New York: SUNY Press.

7

Camp-Parent Partnerships = Parent-Camp Loyalty

by David Lira Leveron

Camp-parent partnerships reach beyond customer satisfaction; they are at the core of parent-camp loyalty. In most Hispanic communities, the camp-parent partnership becomes a critical alliance that often originates at the camp and is based on the mutual fulfillment of needs. This is especially true for nonprofit camps serving underprivileged minority clienteles where partnerships are crucial for the mere existence of the camp.

In our quest for customer satisfaction, we fulfill campers' needs by providing a fun, secure, and nurturing environment. We also fulfill parents' needs by reassuring them about safety concerns, providing growth opportunities and skills development for their children, and making sure that our parents know that we are constantly making efforts to understand their culture and adjusting our approaches and philosophy to meet their needs. Parents and campers fulfill our camps' needs by providing important feedback, return business, word-of-mouth advertising, and by providing the camp with a prominent position in their communities, which can translate into greater funding potential for us.

Loyalty is more. It is the direct result of strong relationships that go beyond partnerships, and although it is mutual, it usually originates with the camper and subsequently includes the parent. Loyalty is the parent's conviction that our camp has made the commitment to go the step beyond fulfilling needs to embrace his or her child and the family's culture as part of our camp's community. More often than not, the camp director is at the forefront of this delicate and important task. He acts as moderator between campers, parents, higher echelons of the organization, and finally the board of trustees.

An 80-Year History

The Union League Boys and Girls Clubs (ULBGC) Camp is a nonprofit agency camp. Located in southeastern Wisconsin, it serves campers from three different ethnic neighborhoods in Chicago: Pilsen, West Town, and Humboldt Park. For over eighty years, the camp, which is owned and operated by the Union League Boys and Girls Clubs, has been providing services to underprivileged children. As a beacon of outdoor programs in our communities, the camp has created many important partnerships, especially with the parents in the communities that it serves.

Of the 512 campers that attend camp each summer, about 97 percent are children who belong to ethnic minorities (63-percent Hispanic and around 34-percent African American). The priorities, in the past, for these populations have not included sending their kids to camp during the summer. However, the camp's success in forming strong partnerships has helped parents in these communities re-examine their priorities—now they are putting summer camp as a top item on their list of summer activities. Without a doubt this is the result of an overall camp strategy that has involved the untiring efforts of a committed board of trustees (through an active camp committee and various subcommittees), a visionary executive director, and the tireless work of a team of summer-camp staff that strongly believe in the importance of the camp experience, the value of loyalty, and the significance of strong community partnerships.

A Worthy Challenge

Creating strong camp-parent partnerships in our communities has not been an easy task. It requires a constant exchange of information that moves upward from the campers to the board and downward from the board to the campers. While passing through the different points in between, (camp director, executive director, and different subcommittees) the information is received, interpreted, discussed, and shaped into the strategies that have helped create not only great camp-parent partnerships but also legendary loyalty that has campers and former campers coming back to camp year after year.

Communication

In 1995, we asked parents to share one of their greatest concerns about sending their children to camp. Their reply was that they could not communicate with their children while at camp. Because our boys and girls clubs operate in heavily Hispanic populated neighborhoods, we understood that concern and created a policy to address it. Even though we rarely allow campers to call home, we allow parents to call their children during mealtime. It is a welcomed courtesy that parents of first-time campers appreciate and use extensively.

The most interesting outcome of this unique communication policy is that by the second season, parents call fewer times than the first and by the third they stop calling entirely. As the first strategy that demonstrated the camp's commitment to serve parents and campers beyond customer service and satisfaction, it has helped cement a sense of trust for the next eleven years that has translated into more Hispanic parents sending their children to camp.

Visits

The next time we asked for feedback from parents, their concerns focused in one of our original policies that restricted parents from visiting their children at camp. Our challenge was to convince parents from inner-city Chicago, mainly first generation Hispanics, that the camp was a fun, safe, and positive place for their children. We realized that by not allowing them to visit the camp, the level of trust was not there. If they were not allowed to visit their children at camp, they were not going to send them.

In a drastic change of policy in 1996, we decided to implement an open-door policy for all parents who wished to visit their children at camp. With the implementation of this policy, we have seen an increase in satisfied parents who feel part of our camp community and in control of what's going on in the lives of their children.

Every weekend at the middle of each session, parents are welcomed to visit their children at camp. Many of them take their kids out of campgrounds for the afternoon and when they bring them back, campers seem to be more relaxed and ready for the following week. Parents leave camp convinced that everything is OK.

Each Sunday afternoon in the middle of the session, we have a giant cookout. Many parents drive more than 60 miles to come to camp to help at the grills and to serve the food. It becomes a family event—a community event. The open-door policy also provides parents the opportunity to bring clean clothes for their children, bring boxes full of goodies, and most importantly, meet personally with the cabin counselors, the unit leaders, and the camp director. It is partnership building at its best.

When some parents indicate that they cannot make the decision to send their children to summer camp because they have not seen the camp, the camp and the clubs make it possible for the parents who lack transportation to visit the camp. In some limited instances, when mothers show concern about their children attending summer camp, we provide transportation and invite them to visit the camp with their children. The Boys and Girls Clubs have gone as far as taking groups of parents during the months preceding the summer camp season to visit the camp and have offered summer camp programs like campfires, songfests, etc., at the clubs during the off-season to familiarize parents and club members with the camp and all it offers. These efforts have had a tremendous effect in the way parents in our communities view our program and have strengthened the relationships between parents and staff.

Parent Volunteers

Some parents, although they recognized the value of the camp experience for their children, had never been away from their children for such an extended period of time. They asked if they could work as a volunteer at the camp when their child was there. Again, we were confronted with a situation that needed special attention. How many parents should we allow to volunteer? What should be the extent of their involvement?

Increased Community Outreach

As more parents discover the positive impact of the camp experience, we realize an increase in both public education and public relations on the benefits of summer camp. For example, for the last two years the Department of Multilingual and Multicultural Programs of the Chicago Public Schools has invited the Union League Boys and Girls Clubs Camp to make presentations about our summer camp programs to more than 200 parents representing all the Chicago Public Schools. This is a definite product of the partnerships that the camp has created over the years with satisfied and loyal parents. Additionally, for five years, the ULBGC Camp in partnership with ACA, Illinois has held camp informational fairs in five Chicago Public Schools during report-card pick-up day. This year, we increased the number to 10 grammar schools.

As we move forward in our quest to serve the disadvantaged children living in our Hispanic and African American communities, it is clear that we will experience more parent concerns. We are already preparing for these concerns. For example, in November 2005, our Camp Program Subcommittee invited a group of campers of different ages and genders, and from different neighborhoods, to come to meet with our board and evaluate the last summer's program together. The outcome was outstanding. Not only did the campers feel that they had a say in the development of the program, but parents thought that inviting their children to be part of the process was an important step. Additionally, the subcommittee had the opportunity to make sound recommendations that will impact the delivery of camp programs for years to come.

The next step is to hold parent forums designed to encourage direct response and to learn more about their concerns, ideas, and expectations. We are continuously looking for new strategies that will increase our parents' sense of comfort with our approaches. Our camp team is committed to developing partnerships with other organizations that offer outstanding programs designed to improve the quality of life in underprivileged communities. We have partnered with FirstPic Inc., the Office of Justice Programs, and Immersion Presents to implement a crime-prevention program while teaching campers about science and technology.

Our camp brochures are bilingual (written in both English and Spanish) and some summer staff are recruited from the same neighborhoods from which our clientele come. Parents are offered the opportunity to volunteer and visit the camp and are constantly reminded of the importance of camp-parent partnerships. The camp director makes sure that the camp maintains a strong presence in the schools where most of our campers attend.

The Future Looks Bright

The future looks bright for the Union League Boys and Girls Clubs Camp, yet we remain vigilant to the many challenges that might arise in our pursuit for excellent service. Our commitment is to serve our campers beyond just customer satisfaction and to create strong partnerships with their parents and the communities in which they live. Olga Gonzalez-Granat, an educator at the Valparaiso, Indiana, school district summarized our core camp philosophy—one that we've been practicing for years: "The Golden Rule is out. No longer are you expected to treat people the way you wish to be treated. The new rule is: Treat people as they wish to be treated."

8

Recruiting Latino Youth to Participate in Resident Camps

by Mario Magaña, M.A., Maureen Hosty, M.A., and Beverly B. Hobbs, Ph.D.

Challenges

Latinos are the fastest-growing minority group in the United States and face unique problems relevant to language and culture. As the Latino population in the United States continues to grow, youth-serving agencies including camp organizations are challenged to find new avenues through which education and recreation programs can be delivered to this group. However, many organizations do not know how to best reach out to Latinos, what programs are needed, or how to deliver programs to this group.

Oregon is characteristic of many states where the Latino population is rapidly increasing. According to Duarte & Castillo (2006), Latinos are the largest ethnic population in the state representing over 11 percent of the state's population, with over 383,925 Latinos. Between 1990 and 2000, the number of Latinos in the state grew by 144 percent, one of the top ten-fastest growing Latino populations in the nation. In the Portland metropolitan area alone, the number of Latinos increased by 191 percent to 161,831 in the last ten years.

The Oregon 4-H youth program sought to identify the factors that discourage Latino youth's participation in camp and to design and implement a camp that would attract these youth. As a result, the 4-H Latino Olympic Summer Camp was developed in an effort to address these issues and to help Latino youth gain skills, knowledge, and attitudes that will prepare them for self-directing, contributing, and productive lives.

This article describes some of the challenges and barriers in recruiting Latino youth for camp and strategies used to overcome these barriers in establishing the Oregon 4-H Latino Olympic Summer Camp. Its focus is on the process we used to create a resident summer camp that has enjoyed great success in engaging Latino middle school youth.

Barriers to Participation

Camp programs that reach out to Latino youth face many barriers at multiple levels. Each of these barriers must be addressed if Latino youth and families are to be reached.

The Influence of Personalism and Familism

Personalism and familism are key values present in the Latino culture. Personalism refers to the faith in person-to-person contact. In other words, there is no substitute for face-to-face interaction. Camp staff needs to personalize their recruitment in reaching out to the community. Familism refers to the central position that the family holds in the life of the individual. All decisions by the individual are made with regard to the well-being of the family. As a result, sometimes parents tend to be overprotective of their children, especially girls, thereby limiting their children's ability to "expand their horizons" (Marsiglia, 1990). In the Latino culture where the family unit is valued and important, it also means an invitation to one family member is an invitation to the entire family. Camp staff recruiters need to be sensitive to Latino parents' concern that allowing their child to attend an overnight experience without the entire family may be unsafe.

Personalism and familism also play a very important role in how camp programs are designed. Latino parents have concerns about cultural differences, values, manners, and religion where most of the campers are non-Latino. Parents are afraid that their children might face discrimination or put-downs. Parents need the assurance that the camp provider understands the value of the person-to-person interaction with their children and that the parents themselves should be considered the central influence in the child's life.

Concerns About Overnight Stays

An overnight camp experience is a tradition that is not embraced by the Latino culture as it is among traditional camp audiences. Even the popular "overnight stays" and "slumber parties" are not common among the Latino families. Slumber parties are hard to understand even for second and third generation Latinos. Overnight stays with friends are not a part of or accepted by Latino culture. Gaining the involvement of Latino families in camp often takes dedicated staff time. Latino involvement is premised on establishing personal relationships with Latino parents and developing a level of trust, two very time-consuming tasks (Hobbs, 2000).

Limited Understanding of the Value of Camp

The majority of Latino parents do not have a camp experience themselves either in the United States and/or in their country of origin. Some parents have a limited education and do not understand how camp can benefit their children. Furthermore, many parents are monolingual Spanish speakers and camp organizations often do not have staff who can explain details about the camp experience in Spanish. Organizations also seldom provide printed informational materials in Spanish. Latino families place a high value on education, yet Latinos tend to have less education than other ethnic groups (Caudle, 1993). Camp programs that emphasize the educational benefits and challenging academic opportunities of camp will go a long way in effectively recruiting Latino youth and families. Having professional bicultural and bilingual staff that can assist with recruiting and meeting with Latino families and highlighting the educational benefits of camp is an important step in helping parents recognize the value of camp.

Limited Financial Resources

In Oregon, approximately 72 percent (103,118) of Latino children live in low-income families compared with 31 percent (188,673) of white children, and 38 percent (54,615) of Latino children live in poor families compared with 12 percent (69,597) of white children (National Center for Children in Poverty [NCCP], 2006). Many children in the state of Oregon do not participate in activities in out-of-school time because they lack financial resources to pay for costs that are associated with participation. In most cases Latino youth will not be able to participate in a summer camp without a camp scholarship.

Transportation

Lack of transportation is another challenge facing Latino families. Many families own only one car, and in most families, just the adult male drives. As a result, many Latino youth have no transportation to get to the camp or even a camp bus pick-up location. The Oregon 4-H Latino camp had to reject many children who wanted to participate simply because their parents could not provide transportation, and there was no budget for transportation to pick up the children at their homes. While some community organization partners were available to help transport children to camp, not all children who wanted to attend camp received transportation assistance.

The Digital Divide

Local needs assessments identified Latino youth and families as underserved audiences in a number of counties in the state. National assessments have drawn attention to the fact that a "digital divide" is evident between those people who are technologically adept and those who are technologically illiterate. Many of those who lack technological skills have low-income levels and fewer learning opportunities, characteristics shared by most Latino youth and families in Oregon. As more and more camps turn to Internet-based registration, promotion, and communication, the Latino population may be largely left behind.

The Oregon 4-H Latino Olympic Summer Camp

The Oregon 4-H Latino Olympic Summer Camp is designed to help Latino youth develop the skills, knowledge, and attitudes they will need to succeed in life. 145 middle school Latino campers and 38 high school Latino counselors participated in the five day resident camps in 2004 and 2005. A key component of the project plan was to help Latino students understand the importance of education and to encourage them to finish high school and plan for post secondary education. In addition, they had the opportunity to meet new friends with a positive vision and attitude towards the future, meet professional people who could be resources in the future, and meet other Latino role models from the community.

Volunteer professionals from universities, private businesses, and community organizations provided a varied menu of workshops focused specifically on technology, natural resources, health, and the arts. Evening programs highlighted successful professional Latino speakers who provided motivational speeches on the importance of finishing high school and how to pursue a college career. Presenters and speakers also talked about the many careers in natural resources, technology, health professions, education, business, etc. A robust schedule of sports activities and traditional camp events rounded out the program. An emphasis on reinforcing Latino culture was apparent throughout the camp.

At the end of camp in 2005, campers (n = 71) and counselors (n = 17) participated in reflective end-of-camp surveys evaluating their camp experiences. Campers gave the camp high marks for life-skill development in eight life-skill areas including cooperating with others, working as a team, and learning responsibility (Sawer & Magaña, 2005).

Campers also reported significant and positive changes when asked to reflect on how they felt before and after their camp experience in terms of meeting new friends, being away from home overnight, and developing a love for nature. When asked what they liked best about camp, campers focused mostly on sports and recreational opportunities (swimming, archery, soccer, dancing, etc.). Counselors reported numerous gains in personal development as a result of their counseling experience. In a separate survey, the counselors were asked to indicate how much they agreed or disagreed that their counseling experience had contributed to their personal development in 18 specific areas. Counselors reported gains in all 18 areas (Sawer & Magaña, 2005).

Steps to Create a Culturally Responsive Camp

The following is a list of suggestions for designing an effective camp, one that will meet the needs and interests of Latino youth.

Personalize the Camp Program

- Plan and design a culturally appropriate agenda for the camp's program. An educational component should be the number one priority on the agenda. This component will attract parental support. The camp director, staff, and counselors must relate and understand the language and culture to be able to answer critical questions posed by parents when they have concerns about their children's safety. Keeping in mind that the camp is for Latino children, provide culturally appropriate and appealing activities with the sole purpose of attracting Latino youth. Sports such as soccer, swimming, canoeing, and archery are sports that attract Latino youth. Fun activities such as dance, treasure hunting, water balloons, campfire, etc., are also appealing.

- All messages delivered to Latino audiences must be culturally attuned (Segal & Sosa, 1983). Insufficient attention to cultural considerations will have adverse affects on the positive aspects of camp. A native Spanish-speaking editor should write, or at least proofread, all informal resources, print ads, and flyers for language and cultural considerations. The camp's flyer, agenda, and program have to show its purpose and relate to the target audiences. For example, help parents understand the goals of the camp and the responsibilities of the participating youth. Develop a camp promotional flyer showing a child playing soccer, the most popular Latino sport.

- Camp staff need to be culturally sensitive and where possible, bicultural and bilingual. Not all staff will be required to be bicultural and bilingual, but especially in the early years of developing a program that reaches out to Latino youth, staff reflective of the community will help build a strong base of support. Latino volunteers who can help are not too difficult to find if you have created some trust in the community. The best way to recruit volunteers is by extending personal invitations either in face-to-face meetings or by calling them by phone. For those who use email, an email message may also work. Sharing the camp information in meetings, churches, organizations, agencies, and schools will also help to recruit youth and adult volunteers.

Plan and Train

- Create a local Latino Camp Council with other professionals who have camp experience. Invite people from the community with experience or interest in helping to provide educational camp experiences for Latino youth. Make sure that everyone who is invited plays at least one role in the camp's planning.

- Training Latino adult and youth volunteers is very important. It prepares the volunteers for unexpected events, so they will be ready to handle the problems or look for the proper help as needed. Offer at least one or two trainings on site so that camp counselors, volunteers, and staff will have knowledge of the trails, roads, and facilities. It should be noted that some adult Latino volunteers may need to have the training delivered in Spanish. Relying on demonstrations and oral presentation as teaching methods as opposed to written materials will accommodate volunteers with limited formal education. Also, include information in the training about the organization and how volunteers contribute.

Identify Funding Sources

- Funding is the most critical factor in delivering a summer camp for Latino youth, since many youth cannot afford the cost of camp. As previously mentioned, it will be necessary to provide camp scholarships for many potential campers. Latino businesses, government agencies, and public agencies are good sources of financial and transportation support. It will be important to prove that you have staff to implement the program and Latino family support in order to convince donors to contribute money for a summer camp. Look for people who already have established strong relationships with potential grantees to advocate for you. Many businesses and organizations will donate if they can collaborate with other agencies and organizations that have the same vision. The Latino Camp Council may also be able to suggest funding sources or even secure those funding sources.

Communicate Your Message

- Though the Internet may be a good way to promote camp to traditional audiences, promoting a Latino camp is most effective when it's done through schools, churches, and other youth organizations. Be sure to contact other professionals working with youth. Radio and television are major forces in marketing educational programs because they reach large segments of the target audience at different times of the day in a variety of places. In particular, radio is a proven medium for distributing information in Latino cultures, and those camp providers who want to have Latinos as part of their target audience should utilize this medium (Cudaback, Marshall, & Knox, 1994). The best and most economical way to do this is by writing creative public service announcements and airing those on Spanish and English language radio and television stations. If a contact phone number is provided, be sure that someone from the camp staff who speaks Spanish is available for in-coming calls from Latino families.

A Broader Audience

It is clear when camps are culturally responsive, Latino youth will participate; however, mainstream camps do not always need to create a new camp solely for Latino youth. By incorporating the suggested practices outlined in this article, mainstream camps can become more attractive to Latino youth and families.

As our society becomes more culturally diverse and as the Latino population continues to rapidly expand, camp staff need to explore and adapt to new ways of designing and delivering camp. Camps that reach Latino youth may need to look different and be conducted differently, and sometimes even separately, if camp organizations are truly interested in expanding the audiences they serve. It is important to understand that this does not mean that Latino camps are less of a part of the total camp program. It simply means that camp organizations are becoming more able to provide the camp experience to a broader audience.

References

Candle, P. (1993). Providing culturally sensitive health care to Latino clients. *Nurse Practitioner*, 10(12), 43-51.

Cudaback, D. (1994, December). "The Magic Years: Parent Education by Spanish Language Radio". *Journal of Extension*, 32(4). Article a3. Retrieved July 19, 2006, from http://www.joe.org/joe/1994december/a3.html.

Duarte, A., & Castillo, G. (2006). Latino Metropolitan Chamber: Investing in Oregon's Future. Retrieved July 19, 2006, from http://www.hmccoregon.com/.

Hobbs, B. (2000). *Recruiting and Supporting Latino Volunteers*. Corvallis, OR: Oregon State University Extension.

Marsiglia, F.F. (1990). The ethnic warriors: Ethnic identity and school achievement as perceived by a selected group of mainland Puerto Rican students. Unpublished doctoral dissertation, Case Western Reserve University, Cleveland.

National Center for Children in Poverty (NCCP). State Demographic Profiles. Retrieved July 19, 2006, from http://www.nccp.org/state_detail_demographic_poor_OR.html.

Sawer, B. & Magaña A. M. (2004-2005). Latino Olympic Summer Camp. Unpublished Report. Corvallis, OR: Oregon State University Extension Service.

Segal, M., & Sosa, L. (1983). "Marketing to the Latino Community". *California Marketing Research*, 26(1), 120-134.

9

The Words of the Profits— Highlights From ACA's Camp Business Operations Report: 2006

by Jon Malinowski, Ph.D.

As part of its efforts to better understand the needs of its members, the American Camp Association (ACA) conducts periodic research on business issues, the benefits of the summer-camp experience, and youth development. In November and December 2005, the association funded a major survey on camp business operations. Each of ACA's 2,680 member camps was sent a survey, and 1,097 usable responses were received, a 41 percent return rate. The results indicate that the camp community remains a complicated family with a great degree of diversity among its members.

Resident Camps

Resident camps that responded to the survey consisted of independent camps (36 percent); agency camps (33 percent); and religious camps (24 percent). Among the independent camps, for-profit camps were slightly more represented than nonprofit camps (19 percent of all respondents compared to 17 percent). Among agency camps, the YMCA (11 percent of all respondents) and the Girl Scouts (8 percent of all respondents) were the most commonly represented organizations.

Summer Youth-Camp Fees

Among the responding residential camps, the average weekly fee for summer youth camp was $597. The vast majority of residential camps, approximately 65 percent, charge more than $300 per week for summer camp, and 10 percent reported fees of $1,000 per week or more. Only 7 percent of respondents reported fees of under $100 per week. As shown in Figure 1 below, New England has the highest median summer camp registration fees, at $780 per week, while the Mid-America states have the lowest at just $325 for the median fee. The term median means that 50 percent of camps are below and 50 percent of camps are above this number.

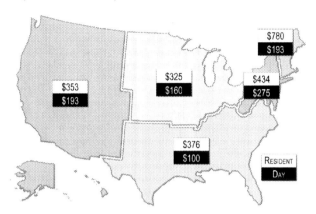

Not surprisingly, independent for-profit camps were most likely to report high weekly fees. Nearly 42 percent of independent for-profits reported fees above $1,000 per week, and another 42 percent indicated fees between $700-$999. Among agency-affiliated camps, only 2 of 223 respondents indicated fees above $1,000 per week, a number well under 1 percent. Similarly, only 2 percent of religious-affiliated camps and 4 percent of independent nonprofit residential camps reported weekly fees above $1,000 for camp. Overall, the average weekly fees by sponsor were $377 for agency-sponsored camps, $566 for religious-sponsored camps, $457 for independent nonprofits, and $952 for independent for-profits.

Because of the camp community's roots in service, camps continue to be generous givers of scholarships to campers or other guests at their facilities. Of the residential camps responding, the average amount given in scholarships during the relevant fiscal year was nearly $68,000 and the median was $17,000. Again, this means that 50 percent of respondents awarded more than $17,000 in scholarships, and 50 percent awarded less than $17,000. Independent nonprofit residential camps were the most likely to report scholarships of over $100,000 or more. Nearly 27 percent of respondents in this category reported doing so. Independent for-profit camps were most likely to report no scholarships. About 21 percent of camps in this category reported no scholarships, compared with just 10 percent of agency residential camps, 8 percent of religious-sponsored camps, and 8 percent of independent nonprofits.

Noncamp Services and Months of Operation

A large number of residential camps reported offering services other than summer youth-camp programs. Over 40 percent of respondents indicated that they offered a retreat center, family camp programs, or outdoor/environmental-education programs. Furthermore, over 30 percent of all residential camps offer weekend or daily rentals, site rental by other camps, day-use programs, or trip and/or travel camp. Finally, about 25 percent of all residential camps reported conference-center or day-camp services. Regionally, retreat centers were least common in New England and most common in the Mid-Atlantic and Mid-America regions. Family camp services were most common in the Mid-America and Western regions.

These findings suggest that a typical residential camp is much more than just a "summer" camp, and other aspects of the survey seem to prove this. As expected, over 90 percent of all residential camps report being in operation during June, July, and August, but the other months of the year are not being neglected. Over 40 percent of resident camps report operations in January, February, March, and November, over 50 percent are operating in April and October, and over 60 percent operate in May and September. December is the least common month for operation, but even then a full 39 percent of camps reported operating. As might be expected, New England residential camps report the lowest winter operations, with only 13-16 percent of all camps in operation. Perhaps this shorter reported operating season is one reason that weekly summer-camp fees are higher in the New England states.

Gross Revenues

Respondents to the survey were asked to report an estimated gross revenue in their current fiscal year from all sources. The average for residential camps was $961,000 and the median was $540,000. Approximately 13 percent of camps reported estimated total gross revenues of over $2 million and 16 percent estimate between $1-1.9 million. At the other end of the spectrum, 8 percent of camps estimate gross revenues of under $100,000 for the year. New England residential camps reported the highest estimated total gross revenues, at $1.2 million. Mid-Atlantic residential camps reported the next highest median estimated revenues at $624,000, followed by Southern camps at $560,000; Mid-America camps at $400,000; and Western camps at $331,000.

Well over half of all revenue reported by residential camps, nearly 59 percent, comes from summer camp-registration fees. After these fees, group rental fees and contributions each account for about a tenth of the respondent camps' gross revenues. New England camps seem to be the most dependent on camp-registration fees. In these states, nearly 76 percent of revenue comes from this source. Also, and as is to be expected, independent for-profit camps rely more heavily on camper-registration fees. Over 89 percent of the revenue for independent for-profits was estimated to come from camper fees, compared to just 45 percent for independent nonprofit residential camps.

Residential Camp Expenses and Profitability

Labor is the largest expense for residential camps according to the respondents, accounting for 40 percent of outlays. The next single largest expense reported was food, at 11.4 percent of expenses, and program items and supplies, at 8.3 percent of all costs. Maintenance and insurance were the next largest expenses. Overall, average estimated expenses reported by residential camps were $896,000, with a median of $530,000. Independent for-profit camps have the highest expenses of all camp types, with average outlays of nearly $1.4 million. This was substantially higher than independent nonprofits ($955,000); agency-sponsored residential camps ($782,000); or religious-sponsored residential respondents ($638,000). New England camps have estimated median expenses that are over $350,000 higher than those of residential camps in any other region.

Based on the data provided by survey respondents, a simple measure of profitability was calculated by subtracting expenses from revenue. Overall, 19 percent of residential camps show no "profit"; 46 percent show a profit; and 25 percent of residential camps show a loss. Among camps that show a profit, 13 percent had returns of $300,000 or more, and 24 percent had profits of $100,000-$299,999. This means that the vast majority of camps showing a profit, nearly 63 percent, generated returns of less than $100,000. Among residential camps that reported expenses greater than revenues, nearly 19 percent had calculated losses of over $100,000, 49 percent had deficits of between $10,000 and $99,999, and 20 percent showed losses of less than $10,000.

Day Camps

A total of 305 day camps participated in this study. About 43 percent of the camps were agency sponsored, and the vast majority of these camps are affiliated with the YMCA. Approximately 37 percent of the day camps participating are independent, divided roughly equally among for-profit and nonprofit entities. Religious-sponsored camps constituted just 6 percent of the respondents. Municipal or government day camps (7 percent) and day camps in multiple categories rounded out the respondents. Agency-sponsored day camps were more commonly from the Western or Mid-America regions while the New England and Mid-Atlantic states had more independent programs. Municipal- or government-sponsored day camps were more common in Southern states than in other regions.

Summer Youth Camp Fees

As expected, weekly fees for day camps are lower than for residential camps. Approximately 66 percent of day camps charge between $100-299 for a week. Only 3 percent of all day camps responding reported fees of over $700 per week. Overall, the average fee for a week at one of the participating day camps was $303. Agency-sponsored day camps reported the lowest average fees, at just $157, followed in order of increasing cost by religious-sponsored programs ($222); independent for-profit camps ($494); and independent nonprofit camps ($570). The fact that nonprofit camps have higher average fees is skewed a bit by a few programs with high fees. The median fees are $230 for the nonprofit programs and $400 for the for-profit day camps. Thus, while nonprofits have higher average day-camp fees, the bottom 50 percent of day camps in this category charge less than the bottom 50 percent of camps in the for-profit category. Regionally, as shown in Figure 1, median weekly fees were highest in the Mid-Atlantic states ($275); followed by the New England and Western states ($193); the Mid-America states ($160); and the Southern states ($100).

In terms of scholarships, agency-sponsored camps report the highest level of giving, with a median amount of $14,600. Religious-sponsored day camps and independent for-profit camps both had median scholarships of $10,000, and independent nonprofits indicated median scholarships of $5,000. Overall, 100 percent of religious, 98 percent of agency, 80 percent of for-profit independent, and 77 percent of independent nonprofit day camps provide scholarships.

Noncamp Services and Months of Operation

Day camps are less likely than residential camps to offer other services beyond youth camp programs. The most common services offered were outdoor- or environmental-education programs (23 percent of respondents); trip or travel camp (23 percent); and day-use programs (22 percent). Site rentals, community centers, and daily rentals were reported by 7-9 percent of the respondents.

Given these findings, it's not surprising that we see a more limited calendar of operations for most day camps (see Figure 2 on page 19). While 93-99 percent of all day camps were in operation during June, July, and August, in no other month did the percentage of day camps in operation crack 30 percent. April, May, and September were operating months for between 25-29 percent of day camps, and all other months were only times of operation for between 16-24 percent of responding day camps. Thus, "summer camp" is a much more accurate term for most day-camp programs than for residential programs that more commonly offer services beyond youth camp programs over the course of the year.

Gross Revenues

With their lower weekly fees, it's not surprising that day camps have lower gross revenues than residential camps. The average gross revenue for the participating day camps was $637,000, but half of all day camps reported revenue of less than

$268,000. Independent for-profit camps have the highest grosses, averaging $1.6 million. Independent nonprofits reported average revenues of $615,000, followed by religious day camps ($600,000) and agency-sponsored programs ($274,000). Geographically, Mid-Atlantic camps reported the highest gross revenues, $600,000, and Southern camps indicated the lowest figures, just $60,000.

Because day camps offer fewer programs other than youth camp programs, it's not surprising that revenue for day camps comes largely from camper registration fees. In fact, the day-camp respondents to this survey reported that over 80 percent of their gross revenue comes from camper fees. No other single source accounts for even 5 percent of the average gross revenues of the responding camps. This makes day camps particularly vulnerable, when compared to residential camps, to economic, social, or legal issues that might reduce camp enrollment. For most day camps, a 10 percent reduction in enrollment translates to about an 8 percent loss of revenue. For the residential camps participating in this survey, that loss would be more in the range of just 6 percent of revenue.

Day Camp Expenses and Profitability

Day camps spend a higher percentage of their budgets on labor (54 percent) compared to residential camps (40 percent). Program supplies and transportation costs are the next largest single budget items, accounting for 10.2 percent and 7.6 percent of expenses, respectfully. Overall, day camps in this study reported average expenses of $522,000. Independent for-profit camps have the highest expenses, averaging nearly $1.4 million, followed by religious day camps ($588,000); independent nonprofits ($461,000); and agency programs ($230,000). Reported expenses were highest in the Mid-Atlantic region and lowest in the Southern states.

As defined as revenue minus expenses, only 13 percent of the day camps participating show a loss while 60 percent indicate a profit. Nearly 21 percent of all day camps in the study report profits of over $100,000. Conversely, only 2 percent of all day camps have an estimated loss of over $100,000.

Conclusion

In addition to providing statistics about the operating status of current ACA members, this study highlights the diversity of the association's membership. Expenses and revenue vary widely by camp type (day or resident); camp sponsor (agency, independent, etc.); and geographic location. Because of this, the national and regional leadership of the association must continue to carefully evaluate the needs of all members and to work together to insure that national policies meet regional and local needs whenever possible.

10

The Role of Safety

by Marge Scanlin, Ed.D., Pat Smith, June Gray, Phil DeLong, Joe Van Tassel, and Sandra Publicover

We've all heard the story of Chicken Little. The falling acorn had Chicken Little convinced that the sky was falling. She gathered Henny Penny, Goosey Poosey, and Turkey Lurkey to go and tell the king. A silly little fable. Perhaps, but it is telling that there are several versions to the fable. Some have Foxy Loxy luring the little band away never to be heard from again, while other versions have the king's hounds and hunters arriving to scare away the fox and save the day, and still other versions have the smart fox pointing out to Chicken Little what was really happening.

Whatever moral you may draw from the story, consider the truth that perceptions create their own reality. Many camp directors perceive camp as safe. After all, there are accreditation standards, risk-management plans, safety regulations, and certifications for staff, but those things are invisible to campers and do not, in and of themselves, create a safe environment for youth. Campers come to camp with a duffle bag full of hopes and fears, of uncertainties and concerns about whether they will make friends and be accepted, and whether they will be physically and emotionally safe.

Eighty camp directors who participated in the ACA Youth Development Benchmark Survey in 2004 learned that campers perceive safety quite differently from camp administrators. When asked if they agreed with statements such as "I feel safe when I am at this camp" and "I feel respected by the staff at this camp," only one-third of the campers responded in ways that demonstrate they are consistently reporting the presence of the important elements of physical and emotional safety.

Michelle Gambone, president of Youth Development Strategies, Inc. (YDSI) (ACA's partner in this study), indicates that "a sense of safety is basic and critical to youth. Its absence can have profound effects on their choices and decisions . . . . When young people do feel safe, they are less likely to participate in too many high-risk behaviors that can derail or delay healthy development (Innovations 2006)."

In a 2006 issue of *Camping Magazine*, the Community Action Framework for Youth Development (Gambone, Klem, & Connell, 2002) was briefly described. This framework starts with looking at where we want youth to be as adults: economically self-sufficient, able to sustain healthy family relationships, and contributors to their community. For these outcomes to be achieved, youth need to receive healthy and continuous doses of four critically important supports and opportunities:

- Multiple supportive relationships with adults and peers
- Physical and emotional safety
- Challenging and engaging activities and learning experiences
- Meaningful opportunities for involvement and membership

We learned that camps did extraordinarily well in providing multiple supportive relationships and with intentional efforts were able to increase youth reports of supportive relationships. This article explores issues of safety and some lessons learned by the PIP camps that all staff may want to consider.

The Challenges of Safety

Camp directors were surprised (not pleasantly) that campers' perception of safety was quite different from their own. Within the 23 PIP camps, 41 percent of campers reported optimal levels (meaning they were consistently receiving this support in camp) of physical safety, and 61 percent of campers reported optimal levels of emotional safety. When looking at safety overall (where campers needed to report optimal levels of both emotional and physical safety), only 32 percent of campers were in the optimal category. These results mirrored findings from the benchmark study ACA conducted in 2004 with 80 camps and 7,600 youth. In that larger group, optimal levels of safety were reported by only 30 percent of youth. While this result in camps resulted in a higher percentage than is reported by youth in other types of school and after-school programs, directors were not satisfied. What caused these safety concerns?

Camp directors consistently perceived, in the spirit of Chicken Little, that their campers would report high levels of safety. However, pointed discussions with campers revealed that there were aspects of the camp experience that were unsettling for youth: a new environment with new people. It was beyond the familiarity of their home and school.

Sandra Publicover of Camp Winnetaska, an agency camp in Massachusetts, reported, "In our day camp, we had plenty of safety rules in place. After all, we are Girl Scouts through and through, but we hadn't paid enough attention to the two hours girls may spend on the bus each day. We knew we could do better at creating a safe environment on the bus and greeting them on arrival—being sure no one was alone. We worked to create inclusiveness, a welcome atmosphere, and respect for everyone." All of these efforts go to creating that envelope of emotional safety.

Those thoughts were echoed by Phil DeLong and Joe Van Tassel at Camp Gray, a religiously affiliated camp in Wisconsin. To create this sense of a safe place, they developed "The Big 5—The Firm Foundation". These principles were painted in circles on the dining-room floor, were posted throughout camp, and became the preamble to each cabin's written contract that was established by campers each week.

Camp Gray's Big 5

1. Respect—for yourself, for others, for creation, for others' property, for sacred space at camp

2. Safety—watch out for each other.

3. Relationships—be open to new people and learn how to live together in community.

4. Commitment to growth—learn about yourself, others, new skills, and let others grow at their own pace.

5. Fun—have a positive attitude and be open to having fun and being surprised!

Pat Smith of Camp Wawenock, an independent camp in Maine, indicated that she and directors June Gray, Andy Sangster, and Catriona Sangster focused on the significance of the number of campers who affirmed the importance of their counselors "being there"—in the cabin with them at many times of the day. The older campers said the counselor wasn't really needed for problem solving, but helped them understand the interactions in cabin living. The campers appreciated the relationships and the influence the counselor has on the cabin family group. This is an important part of campers' safety—their counselor helping them to understand the interactions in the group and working closely with the campers.

Other PIP directors indicated they had lots of safety efforts in place, but the campers often didn't understand the rationale for camp rules and procedures. One camp inventoried everyone's belongings on arrival. From the campers' view that was one way to see that they went home with everything they brought to camp, while the camp also saw it as a way to double-check for unsafe things that did not belong in the cabin such as cell phones, weapons, or medications.

Campers did not understand the importance of certified staff, safety equipment, or even rules about bullying. Sometimes these discussions need to be held very deliberately with campers to help them understand the camp community in which they are now immersed.

Making Camp an Even Safer Place

In speaking with directors, two approaches to creating physically and emotionally safe environments were foremost:

1. The quality of the relationships in camp among all campers and all staff

2. The judgment exercised by staff

If we could develop an inoculation to assure these two approaches would occur, we would be millionaires. These simple concepts are quite complex when it comes to making them happen. Intentionality is the key to both. Without intentional planning and efforts to make these two concepts central, they will not happen effectively. In the PIP project, we learned that to create positive change in camp, administrators cannot just address the "weakness" or the "problem" that is identified. There must be a concerted effort to create the change necessary to address these issues across camp structure (S); policies (P); and activities (A)—it's the SPA approach.

The SPA Approach

Let's look at three areas to see how we accomplish the SPA approach to the best of our ability.

Structure as It Relates to Safety

How much staff knows about campers as they arrive is a foundational concept to creating safe environments. All three of the PIP camps described processes for getting to know campers. There are multiple ways to accomplish this task. Don't just pull a single idea and expect it to transform your camp. The important thing is to listen to your campers and staff, and find the structure issues that work for your clientele, site, and philosophy. Some of this work occurs before campers even come to camp. This is a matter of getting information from campers about what they want to do at camp as well as asking parents what they think their campers want to do or need to experience at camp.

Other camps addressed structure by looking at ratios and responsibilities of staff during free time. The addition of supervisors during free time can give staff an opportunity to get to know campers better and to take action on potential situations (such as bullying or exclusion of some of the campers) before they become a problem.

Creating structure from information (knowing about campers before they arrive), supervision (having the right people in place at the right time), and modeling how you want staff to relate to campers is an important first step. Can you say that when each child arrives at your camp someone is ready to greet them and already knows key information about the camper?

Many camps are now requiring camp staff to be present in each resident camp cabin after taps. This step provides an extra level of safety for campers both in moderating behavior and in being immediately available should a problem arise.

Some camps require all camp program staff to live in a cabin. This expectation underscores the family relationship of multiple roles in the family, and everyone caring for each other.

Philosophy and Policy Issues That Relate to Safety

Camp Winnetaska would describe this concept as being sure counselors understand their role. Counselors should not come to camp just to teach horseback riding. They need to come to camp to help youth grow. Riding is the means, not the end.

Camp Gray talked about the culture of their camp program. They hire (or rehire) only those staff who can model the "Big Five" all of the time. These five concepts are not a catchy motto. They are a way of life for every person at camp. These values create a structure that surrounds campers and staff with safety and support. Each decision made in camp is filtered through this structure of values. Can you evaluate every decision or action in camp based on seeing them through the eyes of what your camp values?

Camp Wawenock would say that camp is more than a community, it is a family. We live with our families a long time, and we need to learn how to make them effective units. The camp family, whether a cabin group, unit, or an entire camp, needs to learn to look out for one another the way a good family does. Safety starts and ends in the camp family with every member having a role and a responsibility.

Activities That Relate to Safety

For staff, "activities" are interpreted in this article as those issues that relate to staff hiring and training. First, it is important to recognize that training begins with the interview. The questions you ask and the information you share set the tone for potential employees to understand and experience what is important to your camp. Leaders at Wawenock visit with camp staff during the year, because camp staff is part of the family. We visit family members; therefore, we visit camp staff. We need to learn what is happening with staff. Are their goals changing? What are they learning that has application to camp? What have they been thinking about in terms of improvements at camp or ways they would like to grow through camp experiences? What ideas do they have for the summer?

This interest in your staff is modeling behavior at the most basic level. It establishes camp culture and demonstrates the way relationships between people should happen in camp. The Wawenock directors plan at least three conversations with all staff (new and returning). These conversations reinforce with staff the message to communicate to campers:

- I am important and valued as a person.
- My ideas matter.

Once the administrators place the counselors and staff in this type of relationship, they can expect that the counselors will understand the role they are to have with campers.

PIP directors indicated time and again that staff training does not end once campers arrive. Quality camps have committed themselves to ongoing training throughout the summer. It is challenging to figure out how to maintain safe programs while asking staff to attend additional training. However, it is not reasonable to expect that the 18-21 year old staff (or older) will absorb all the material covered during pre-camp training. Staff need to practice skills (not just hear about them). They need situational experience to develop judgment and maturity. These skills may be accomplished in unit-sized groups rather than the entire staff, but continual practice and reinforcement are the only ways people get better at their jobs.

Directors in the PIP group also talked about the content of staff training. Some camps use staff training to be sure that counselors have activity skills needed to assist or teach programs. The best practice would be to hire staff with technical skills you know are already strong and use staff training to sharpen their teaching skills. For example, how do they handle groups of campers of different ages? How do they establish expectations? How do they motivate the uninterested? How do they help the camper who is afraid or whose skills are well below the other campers in the group? How do staff build skill progression so that mastery is achieved? These types of tasks are the real work of pre-camp training. Staff need to practice teaching scenarios to gain the confidence that they will make wise choices when working with youth.

Basic to All of Us

The number of campers who were optimal in physical and emotional safety was surprisingly lower than camp directors expected. While the percentage of youth in this category was higher in camps than in other youth programs, camps can do even better.

There is much to be gained from going beyond satisfaction surveys as a means to camp evaluation so that we can get at how our staffing and program addresses the need that is basic to all of us: safety (Maslow, 1943). Forty-three percent of the PIP camps significantly improved the percent of youth having an optimal experience in safety at camp in just one year. Many of them were really focused on seeking improvements in other areas we will discuss in subsequent issues: skill-building and youth involvement/engagement.

Before you conclude that "the sky is falling," talk with campers about their experiences at camp. Look at your structure, policies, and activities, and plan some intentional strategies to address safety in camp.

Questions to Ask Campers Before Camp

1. What was the best thing that happened to you this year?

2. What are you most looking forward to doing at camp this summer?

3. What things have changed for you this past year? (New pet, new school, best friend moved away, etc.)

4. What is the most important thing in your life? (Friends, hobbies, family, your faith, your school activities, etc.)

5. What do you want to be called at camp? Do you have a favorite nickname?

Have them email this information back to camp and let each counselor learn important things about their campers before they arrive!

Safety—What Worked?

In the camps where safety improved, some strategies were structural while others involved relationships among staff and campers. Some typical safety strategies were:

*   Installing lights outside cabins, camp entrances, and retreat centers.
*   Ensuring clear, open communication about safety.
*   Having campers participate in setting cabin rules and camp rules and assisting in developing consequences for rule breaking.
*   Having older campers mentor younger campers.
*   Consistently enforcing rules and codes of conduct.
*   Creating up to six camp-wide rules/expectations that are used with all age groups.

Reference

Maslow, A.H. (1943). "A Theory of Human Motivation". *Psychological Review.*

11

Finding Your Niche—Reinventing What a Summer Camp Can Be

by Missy Schenck

The Schenck family purchased the 3,400 acres, now called The Green River Preserve, in the early 1950s as a place to spend weekends and summers fishing, hiking, and exploring the Green River Valley. As a child, Sandy Schenck was fortunate to learn the lore of Green River, not only from his parents, but also from people who had lived in the valley for generations. Newman Levi, a lifelong resident, taught him about tracking, hunting, and valley customs. Charles and Pearl Cox, "an old school" mountain family introduced him to milking cows, churning butter, and cooking on a woodstove. Alfred Heatherly, a logger, and his wife, Lori, taught him stories of Cherokee Indians, jack-o-lanterns, and life in the valley in the early 1900s. From these memorable teachers, he learned a reverence for the land, a sense of valley history, and a joy and wonder of outdoor living. These folks were Sandy's counselors, and he was their camper.

In 1987, Sandy left a career in business to fulfill his lifelong dream of starting a summer camp on the Preserve. After touring camps from Georgia to Maine, Sandy found that the competition for summer camps was intense. If he was going to be successful, he needed a niche. Along the way, a conversation with a child psychologist planted the seed that was to become the Green River Preserve. This psychologist told Sandy about some of the special needs of very bright children.

Schools all over the country had "gifted and talented" programs to meet the needs of this population. Why not design a summer camp specifically for this population? This could be the niche that would set The Green River Preserve apart—to share the magic of this area with campers through a unique, natural science-oriented summer-camp program. Sandy determined that this would be a camp unlike any other, one that not only offers bright and motivated campers the ability to enjoy the freedom the wildlife preserve affords, but also a chance to grow as budding naturalists and individuals. Essentially, Green River reinvented what a summer camp could be.

Strategic Decisions

The strategic decision to design the camp and its programs specifically for bright young naturalists allowed Green River to differentiate itself from other camps. Families with children who are "gifted and talented" recognize the efforts of Green River to provide programs that meet the needs of these children.

Key Components

A key component of Green River is that it is a noncompetitive camp. Perfectionism is an issue particularly relevant to gifted populations. Growing up in an increasingly competitive and stressful world, it is important for our campers to learn healthy and rewarding ways to spend their leisure time. As a result, campers learn skills that they can use for life including rock climbing, fly fishing, canoeing, camping, pottery, and drawing. These fun and noncompetitive skills provide an important outlet for stress relief and for many children, an alternative to competitive team sports.

In a noncompetitive environment, the camp emphasizes self-respect, respect for others, and respect for all living things. For campers and staff, Green River is a "no discount" zone—"put-ups" rather than "put-downs" are encouraged. All campers are afforded a safety net of respect and, consequently, the freedom to truly be themselves. Often, this is very difficult to do in school or "the real world."

The camp promotes the quality of fortitude and encourages campers to be bold and try new activities and build new skills. While other camps offer some of these program components, Green River is careful to consistently apply these principles throughout its entire program. These programming measures allow Green River to better meet the needs of its special population, thus, appealing to a niche market.

The emphasis at Green River is on natural science and experiential learning. The campers are very bright and eager to learn. They want and need more than just entertainment. They need a degree of intellectual stimulation to really feel fulfilled. One unique aspect of The Green River Preserve is the mentor hikes that allow campers to explore with our naturalists the forests, streams, and hidden valleys of the Preserve. Campers learn to use all of their senses to experience the outdoors as they play under waterfalls, crawl into caves, explore archeological sites, track wildlife, and taste edible plants.

Together, campers learn by doing. Our naturalists, whom we call mentors, are men and women of exceptional character who have a genuine love of teaching and the outdoors. All of our mentors are college or masters level graduates with teaching experience—among them are foresters, geologists, biologists, musicians, and professional artists. Our program-wide commitment to experiential learning earned Green River its nonprofit status, not as a summer camp, but as a "wilderness school for gifted children."

The Challenges

There were challenges to implementing that specifically address the needs of gifted populations. The very concept of "gifted" is often misunderstood and difficult to explain. There are so many sizes and shapes of giftedness—children can be gifted academically, linguistically, artistically, musically, scientifically, etc. Green River strives diligently to define its target market population. It is not for everybody. If a child is a bright and eager learner, has age-appropriate social skills, and likes the idea of getting his or her feet wet exploring and learning about the outdoors, this camp may be a very good choice. To qualify for admission to Green River, campers must complete an application, which includes a brief camper essay and a teacher-recommendation form.

Evaluating and insuring that all aspects of Green River's programs are mission compliant is another challenge. All camps face this to some degree, but to specialize in a particular market makes it doubly important to be consistent. For example, camp-wide games of capture the flag are great fun, but to deemphasize competition, the ending score of all games is "fun to fun." Even terms that imply competition are avoided. Consequently, there are no teachers, classes, or swim tests at Green River, only mentors (naturalists), activities, and a swim festival. All administrators and staff of Green River have to be vigilant to stay consistent with the camp mission: "to provide a challenging and nurturing learning experience and to inspire a profound appreciation of interconnectedness, ecological respect, and the joy of living."

Spreading the Word

Looking back over its 19 years, Green River's biggest reason for success was the decision to specialize in a target market. The camp was able to effectively spread the word about its program through a variety of "gifted and talented" educational and advocacy groups. Once parents learned about the program and its design to meet the needs of bright young naturalists, they became enthusiastic supporters of Green River.

The camper population grew quickly and the demand was strong enough to allow us to have tuition comparable to private camps. Consequently, we were able to build outstanding facilities, to offer good staff salaries, and to fund a significant scholarship program.

Special Programs

Green River Preserve offers several special programs above and beyond its traditional summer-camp sessions. By offering these programs, we can extend the Green River Preserve experience throughout the year and to those who may not be able to spend a full summer session here.

Little Tree

One of these programs is Little Tree, which was inspired by Forest Carter's winning novel, *The Education of Little Tree*. School groups in the spring and fall can participate in Little Tree and have the opportunity to gain hands-on experience in natural science, history, and the philosophy of the mountain people. The Little Tree curriculum is interdisciplinary and was written and copyrighted by a group of "gifted teachers" for Green River. School groups read and study Little Tree on their own campus and then come and live Little Tree for a week at Green River. Through this experience students gain a more profound understanding of three themes—cultural heritage, ecological respect, and interconnectedness.

Leadership

The hallmark of Green River is to make a difference in children's lives and to teach young people to be future leaders and better stewards of the land. Through wilderness skills, creative arts, and the exhilaration of outdoor fun and discovery, we strive to inspire young minds. "The people, the land, and the philosophy have shaped my life, and I try each and every day to spread those ideals to others." (camper, Liberty, South Carolina).

12

Post-Incident Risk Management

by Ed Schirick, C.P.C.U., C.I.C., C.R.M.

Managing risk is a year round, 24/7 challenge for most businesses. As we have indicated in the past, the primary goal of risk management is preserving the assets of your organization. The process of identifying, evaluating, controlling, transferring, and monitoring the risk factors that threaten your business is hopefully becoming familiar to camp directors. Camps spend a lot of time and money modifying facilities and educating staff, trying to prevent injuries and damage to property before the campers even set foot on the premises.

Unfortunately, no matter how committed you are to controlling risk in your camp environment and no matter how diligent your training efforts and safety initiatives, incidents occur during camp that damage property or cause injury to campers. Does this mean your risk-management efforts are a failure? Certainly not. Does risk-management end when property is damaged or someone is injured? Definitely not.

Some risk-management professionals prefer to divide their risk-management planning and organizing into two phases. The first part is sometimes referred to as pre-incident (injury) and the second as post-incident (injury) planning. This separation emphasizes the continuous nature of the risk management process and underscores the fact that risk-management doesn't stop after an unexpected or unplanned situation results in injury or damage.

The concept of post-incident risk management is not new, but, some camp professionals may be seeing the term for the first time. Most camps already have some elements of a comprehensive post-incident risk-management plan in place through the use of emergency-action plans and crisis-response plans.

Pre-Incident Versus Post-Incident Risk Management

From my perspective, the main difference is the focus of the activity. In pre-incident risk management, the focus is prevention. In post-incident risk management, the focus shifts to risk and loss reduction.

An excellent example of pre-incident risk management is the training and information directors share with staff during orientation. Directors discuss many things including such prevention issues as following the rules for various activities, and the importance of using personal protective equipment (personal flotation devices while boating, helmets while horseback riding, etc.). An example of post-incident risk management is having systems and procedures in place to allow injured workers who have lost time from work to return to work early in a different capacity.

Cost Reduction is the Goal

The practice of allowing injured employees to return to work earlier than they might have otherwise, doing a different job than the one they did previously, is widely used and accepted as cost effective. In addition, insurance industry experience with workers' compensation claims has demonstrated that the earlier the claim is reported to the insurance company the more cost effectively it is managed. This is a desirable outcome especially if your workers' compensation is experience rated.

The following incident is a case in point. A camp had a maintenance man who was using a gas-powered, grass trimmer with a brush blade attachment to cut thicker grass and weeds at camp. The tool was designed in a way, which prevented, or so they thought, a person from putting their hand near the blade while also keeping pressure on the trigger handle. The flaw in the design was the failure to anticipate that a very tall person, six-foot six or seven, might be able to keep the trigger depressed, bend over, and put their hand near the blade.

This is in fact what happened. The incident occurred in a split second. The injury was severe. The employee nearly severed his hand at the wrist. Fortunately, he received immediate first aid and through the efforts of the camp director had surgery performed to repair the damage to nerves, blood vessels, muscles, and tendons by one of the finest surgeons in the area. He was out of work, undergoing physical therapy, and receiving lost-wages payments from the camp's workers' compensation insurer.

Needless to say, this was a very expensive claim. However, the cost was reduced through an early return-to-work program, which allowed the employee to come back to camp before he was ready to resume maintenance duties and perform other duties. This was done with the approval of his doctors. This approach had a very positive impact on the employee's attitude. Exactly how much money was saved was not quantified, but the insurance company claim department was certain of the benefit to the employee, and other staff, not to mention the camp's loss ratio as a result of this post-incident risk-management technique.

Blind Spots Cause Ineffective Risk Management

This leads to another principle of post-incident risk management. Know and understand your post-incident duties and obligations. These obligations may be imposed upon you by contract (your insurance policy, enrollment agreements, lease agreements, hold harmless and indemnification agreements, etc.), by law, or by your business customs and practices.

Insurance policies are contracts. They impose very specific duties and responsibilities on the policyholder. If you don't know what your obligations are to report incidents, occurrences, accidents, or offenses, take some time this winter to review them with your insurance advisors. The obligations are different for each policy. Knowing your duties and responsibilities and staying involved helps avoid surprises and reduces the risk of taking actions or failing to take actions that might affect insurance coverage or the positive outcome of the situation.

I've spoken to some directors about this issue and have been told they simply rely on their insurance agents and insurance companies to tell them what to do. While this may be convenient, lack of a comprehensive post-incident risk-management plan actually poses additional risk for your organization. Post-incident risk management requires the same amount of time, effort, and attention owners and directors give to pre-incident risk management. This means avoiding the temptation to let your insurance agent and insurance company take care of the matter. This means staying involved until the incident or accident is resolved.

Why Is This Important?

Turning over an incident to your insurance company and expecting them to do the right thing is a little naïve. Most insurance company claim departments are quite expert and capable. However, sometimes the interests of the insurance company and the policyholder differ and unfortunately, every once in a while an insurance company claim department may take some action, such as settle a claim involving no liability, which adversely affects the interests of the policyholder.

A hypothetical case in point is the incident that is reported to the insurance company for records only. Upon receipt in the claim department, a claim is mistakenly established, and without any notice to the policyholder, a settlement is agreed upon with the injured party. In incidents reported for records only, an investigation from the (insured's) camp's point of view would have been appropriate. Contact beyond that with the parents of the injured camper may actually invite a claim. Contact with the parents would have been inappropriate in this example, since no demand had been made for damages. Incidents become claims when there is some demand made for compensation such as a refund of tuition or payment of medical expenses or upon receipt of a letter of representation from an attorney.

You should be aware that when an incident actually becomes a claim, especially when an attorney becomes involved, your involvement will change. Under these circumstances, you must be careful not to interfere with the insurance company's claim-department efforts. This doesn't mean that your interest in the claim ends. It should not. It is reasonable to continue asking for regular updates. You may speak directly with the claim department or work through your insurance agent or broker until the matter is concluded. If the claim involves a lawsuit then the insurance company will assign defense counsel, which changes the dynamic again.

In summary, take some time to review your post-incident risk-management plans and practices. If your risk-management plan doesn't include this focus, reconsider your approach. Determine your duties and obligations imposed by contract, law, and business practice. Consider the risks. Coordinate your planned activity with your insurance agent and insurance company. Cooperate with your insurance company and their representatives handling your camp's incidents, accidents, and claims until they are concluded. Avoid surprises. You can make a difference.

13

Reflections on 2004
and the Road Ahead

by Ed Schirick

Risk-management planning can be done at any time. It is a dynamic, continuous process. Traditionally, fall seems to be a favorite time of year for directors and other business owners to reflect on the past, look forward to the new year, and make plans for the road ahead. Following are some risk-management thoughts about ongoing issues and risk-control measures for consideration in your planning process.

Insurance Marketplace—Availability and Affordability

In 2004, as the underwriting appetites of major underwriters continued to change, camps that served the developmentally disabled, as well as adventure travel programs and U.S.-based programs with operations outside the U.S. and Canada had trouble finding insurance.

The cost of insurance moderated for some in 2004 after a couple of years of double-digit increases in rates and premiums. Umbrella insurance in particular continued to be quite expensive compared to historical average rate formulas.

Some directors found themselves without insurance this summer or with holes in their insurance programs for the first time in many years. Most, but probably not all, found some solutions in the insurance marketplace. Generally, these solutions did not provide the same broad coverage the directors were used to having, and of course, prices were up significantly.

Issue

- Relative instability of the camp-insurance marketplace, with a limited number of specialty underwriters.

Risk Control

Know where you stand with your insurance company.

1. Know your loss history. Get a copy of your loss history every year. Review it carefully and ask questions about any entries that don't seem familiar. Maintain a dialogue with your underwriter through your insurance broker. Find out if there are any old concerns or new issues you should know about before your policies renew. Start at least four months in advance of your insurance policy anniversary date.

2. Don't start any new programs or purchase new equipment, other than replacement equipment, without first running your plans by your underwriter. Paintball wars may sound like a great activity, but may not be very palatable to your underwriter. Investigate their risk appetite before committing your dollars.

3. If your insurance policies typically come due in the late spring or summer, consider changing the dates to the fall, or winter to give yourself more time to re-market your insurance if you have a problem with your insurance for one reason or another.

15-Passenger Vans

The uncertainty surrounding the appropriate use of 15-passenger vans to transport campers and staff continued in 2004. The major U.S. underwriters of camp automobile insurance provided coverage in 2004, but their appetites could change if camps fail collectively to address the fifteen-passenger van's risk management concerns.

Issues

- The relative instability of the vehicle, a design issue with some models, which is exacerbated by the addition of roof racks and trailers to carry equipment;
- Driver experience and judgment amplified by the seasonal nature of the camp business;
- The age of camp automobile fleets;
- Maintenance; and
- Use of seatbelts.

Risk Control

Successful businesses anticipate change and make adjustments before they are forced to do so. Embracing change is critically important when the change is designed to increase the margin of safety.

What can camps do?

1. Markel Insurance Company and other underwriters and risk managers recommend limiting the weight in the vehicle to 75 percent of the manufacturer's recommended Gross Vehicle Weight (GVW). Keep the weight in front of the rear axle if possible.

2. Other guidelines call for prohibiting the use of roof racks and trailers with 15-passenger vans and limiting speed to a maximum of 55 M.P.H. regardless of any higher, posted speed limit.

3. Other risk-control actions include hiring experienced, mature van drivers and offering specific van driver training through an independent contractor or professional driver-training organization.

4. If you own older vans, consider replacing them with the newer models that have been redesigned to improve stability. If you lease, take some time now to find the dealers who can lease you these newer, improved models.

5. Instead of 15-passenger vans, consider using minivans that have received high marks for safety in the crash-worthiness tests conducted by the Insurance Institute for Highway Safety (www.hwysafety.org).

6. Maintain your vehicles regularly according to the manufacturer's recommendations and keep detailed records. Become fanatical about checking the readiness of vehicles daily, paying attention to details such as maintaining proper tire pressure. Establish and maintain high standards like prohibiting the use of any vehicle unless all key operating and safety equipment on and in the vehicles has been checked and found to be satisfactory.

7. We know seatbelts save lives in accidents, but every year it seems someone is injured more seriously or dies because they didn't have their seatbelt on. Insist that everyone riding in camp vehicles wear a seatbelt at all times while the vehicle is in use. No exceptions.

Crisis Readiness

A recent study done by a prominent Connecticut-based insurance company found that many small- and medium-sized businesses in the United States are poorly prepared for a crisis.

Issues

- Many camps have developed emergency-action plans and crisis-response plans and are probably better prepared in some instances than other businesses. However, the blackout experienced by the East Coast toward the end of the summer of 2003 lead many directors to conclude they were not as well prepared as they thought.

- The emphasis on crisis management has been placed on situations involving injury to campers. In addition, these plans tend to focus on immediate short-term issues, leaving property damage and the longer-term business continuation issues often underdeveloped.

Risk Control

Since risk management is a continuous process, it is never too late for you to address issues that threaten the ongoing success of your business. Risk identification, the first step in the risk-management process, is ongoing. As a result, new risks are uncovered, and sometimes, new aspects to previously identified risks are also revealed.

How would your camp continue if something bad happened to the director or owner and their leadership was lost for the summer or permanently? How would camp stay open if the dining hall burned to the ground two weeks before camp was scheduled to open?

1. Take some time during the winter to brainstorm with your key staff about the top-five risks threatening the continuation of your camp business.
2. Develop a plan that responds to each one of the scenarios. Don't forget to include your accountant, lawyer, and insurance advisors in this process.

Criminal-Background Checks and Controlling the Risks of Sexual Misconduct

This is not a new issue. It is continually in the spotlight because the risk is changing. Controlling this risk requires commitment, vigilance, and imagination.

Issues

- It may be hard to believe, but I think there are still some camp directors who have not yet established and committed themselves to a comprehensive plan for screening staff, which includes the best available criminal-background check. This is quite nearsighted and puts their campers, program, and business at great risk.

- Major underwriters of camp liability insurance will continue to focus on criminal background checks to reduce the risk of sexual misconduct between campers and staff. Those with a long-term perspective on this issue recognize that background checks are not a panacea. They are an important addition to an array of other tools, including comprehensive applications for employment, which ask about an applicant's criminal history; personal reference checks; personal interviews; child abuse- and molestation-awareness training for staff; procedures that protect campers and their privacy; and informed, attentive supervision. Directors will not be able to buy insurance for this risk in the foreseeable future unless criminal-background checks are in their staff-screening tool kits.

- There is growing evidence of more sexual misconduct between campers.

Risk Control

Risk management is a continuous process; risks keep changing. In addition, as risk managers study these risks, new methods are developed for managing them. Under these circumstances it is important to keep an open mind and stay focused on constantly improving your organization's risk-management effectiveness.

1. If you haven't made a commitment to criminal-background checks yet, resolve to add them to your staff-screening process before next summer. If you have been doing criminal background checks for some time, take some time this winter to review and update your procedures and practices. What is in your tool kit?

2. Expand your risk management thought process to include the potential for sexual misconduct between campers. Brainstorm this issue with your key staff. Alert your staff to this issue during staff training. Develop risk-control plans that are respectful of camper privacy but reduce the opportunity for this behavior. Some of the same techniques already in your risk-management repertoire may apply to this developing trend.

Invest in yourself and in the long-term success of your business by taking some time to review and update your risk management plan now. Consider these issues and the ongoing and developing risks that you may identify through your risk management process. Maintain your commitment. The risk management discipline is needed now, more than ever.

14

Camps in a World of Change

by Michael Shelton, M.S., C.A.C., C.F.T.

Let's start with a brief cognitive exercise. Imagine that you stop at the local fast-food outlet for lunch (this is not a meal that I am condoning, and as vanguards of youth fitness, we should certainly be more selective in our dietary selections, but for the sake of this imaginary exercise, let's continue on). You place your order at the register and, almost immediately, the manager exits from behind the counter. He hands you an apron and respectfully tells you to go to the grill and start preparing your meal. How would you respond? This is certainly not the expected routine that is supposed to take place at a fast-food establishment. Such an occurrence as described here would likely result in consternation, confusion, bewilderment, and maybe even anger on your part. We hold an internal "map" of what is supposed to happen when we enter a fast-food restaurant and are perplexed when this map is not followed. In fact, we hold thousands of these maps that allow us to proceed through common routines automatically without exerting cognitive effort. Think of these maps as a built-in way the brain conserves energy. We have cognitive maps of the process of, for example, attending a movie theater, using a public bathroom, and visiting a sick person in the hospital. These maps are formed in our youth and are based on our earliest experiences (I can still remember how I learned about being quiet in a movie theater: My mother leaned over and informed me that we do not talk in movie theaters as I happily chatted throughout a showing of *Bambi*).

Hanging on to an outdated model however, no matter how successful it may have been in the past, can lead to far-reaching problems. In the case of the camp industry, the public has an internalized image of summer camp developed either through personal experience or through camp depictions in films. However, in aggregate, these images are either outdated (or for those weaned on camp films, were never accurate to begin with) and do not necessarily match the current reality of summer camps. The American Camp Association (ACA) is making a concerted effort to expand this limited public perception of camp as mere recreational venues through the release of *Directions: Youth Development Outcomes of the Camp Experience*, a study conducted by Philliber Research Associates and ACA. The *Directions* study found scientific evidence that a camp experience produces positive youth development and verifies decades long anecdotal evidence from camp administrators and parents.

The challenge of expanding the public mindset in regards to summer camps is just beginning and will take much effort and must occur at many different levels of the camp industry. However, would it additionally help us in the camp field to examine our own internal working model of camp? All camp administrators have a cognitive map of what a successful camp entails. Maybe it is a lack of problematic children, minimal parental complaints, full coffers, or just a consistent level of fun. Admittedly, all of these are relevant, but we must join with ACA in aspiring to much more, and the first step to change is a thoughtful contemplation of whether our own current cognitive map or model of camp will be able to move us successfully through a world filled with change.

The world is indeed changing, and camps, if they are to be successful, need to change along with it. Some of the changes that we know will affect our future include an aging population, technological breakthroughs, medical advances, and a concurrent catalogue of new diseases that evoke worry. Many in the youth-development field are already preparing for a marked decrease of governmental funding to nonprofits. In addition, these are the changes we can predict with a fair amount of certainty. We have no idea what changes will arise suddenly and unexpectedly (think of the societal changes arising from 9/11).

Famed nature writer Bill McKibben takes an even more macro perspective of the changes likely to occur: "We're not used to the idea that the earth is shifting beneath us. For 10,000 years of human civilization, we've relied on the planet's basic physical stability. Sure, there have been hurricanes, droughts, volcanoes, and tsunamis, but averaged out, it's been a remarkably stable run. Unfortunately, stability is a thing of the past (McKibben, 2006, p. 34)." A great many people would agree with McKibben that our environment is in flux. Therefore, not only do we have to concern ourselves with political, financial, technological, and population changes, the entire world on which we are built is likely also changing. All of this can leave us reeling; it's no wonder why leaders, overwhelmed with the multitude of concurrent change, often have little idea of how to prepare themselves and the businesses they lead.

There is no doubt that the camp industry is already changing and that in order to survive and thrive we will have to accommodate to the changes, expected and unexpected, that society (and the world as a whole) experiences. The remainder of this article focuses on one change that is absolutely necessary if we are to continue to be a successful entity over the next several generations—diversity. Though the value of "diversity" has been reiterated enough times for at least a basic understanding of its importance, there is still a real need to examine and likely modify our existing cognitive map of diversity if we are to work successfully with it.

Diversity Comes to Camp

In 1998, Federal Reserve Chairman Alan Greenspan publicly stated that "Discrimination is patently immoral but it is now increasingly being seen as unprofitable (Halter, 2000, p.46)." Corporations across the country have reaped the financial benefit of diversity marketing. Such corporate luminaries as Hallmark, American Express, Merrill Lynch, J.C. Penny, Mattell, Hasbro, AT&T, and VISA (to name just a tiny number) have all successfully reached out to diverse populations. Indeed, these (and almost all) corporate entities recognize that survival depends very much on positioning themselves as a purveyor of goods and/or services for a heterogeneous population.

An increasingly diversified world is already occurring, will not abate, and is changing the entire fabric of the United States. Some of the factors affecting diversity include immigration, intermarriages (of third-generation immigrants, 41 percent of all Asians and 65 percent of Hispanics marry across group lines), the breakdown of traditional classifications (the strict delineation of black/white/Asian/Hispanic categorization is a relic of the past), and a widespread movement of voluntarily seeking out and celebrating ancestral "roots." These changes have already permeated the boundaries of most camps. For those camp directors that have yet to tackle diversity issues, be certain that within the next several years you will be confronted with the following concerns:

- an aging workforce
- greatly increased Latino, Asian, and immigrant youth
- non-English speaking citizens
- children and adults with chronic health problems and disabilities
- gay and lesbian advocacy
- international staffing

Even ACA's journal *Camping Magazine*, devoted one entire issue to just some of the above-stated challenges (July/August, 2004). The introduction by the CEO eloquently summarized the challenges that camps face in regards to diversity:

> As a parent, I am aware that the world my children will live in will be fundamentally different than the one in which I grew up. I am challenged to appreciate the realities of the new world and how to best prepare my children

to be contributing adults. The depth, breadth, scale, and new face of our world is changing rapidly. Professionally, it also demands that I consider what will be the new face of camp tomorrow. If we feel the camp experience is truly of value to all, then we must understand and be able to serve those new faces of tomorrow (Smith, 2004, p. 15).

Subsequently, the magazine published a series of informative articles on camps in other countries throughout 2005 and continues to impress on leaders the value of diversity. In regards to specific goals, the aforementioned 2004 *Camping Magazine* promulgated several essential considerations for camp administrators:

- The marketing of camps to non-traditional camp populations
- Staffing issues (including demographic changes and recruitment)
- Comprehension and respect of different value systems

It is not an understatement to say that if camps wish to remain viable entities in the future, we must begin to work with the increasingly diverse population of this country.

Two Primary Goals for Diversity

Above all, there are two primary goals for camps concerning diversity:

- To diversify our camps in regards to campers and staff member.
- To manage this diversity for successful outcomes.

Corporations spend millions on marketing, while for many camps (particularly nonprofits), a million dollars is more than double (or triple) the entire yearly budget. Corporations still manage to make some fairly serious (though often amusing) blunders. When Pepsi® began marketing in China, its slogan "Pepsi® Brings You Back to Life" was translated as "Pepsi® Brings Your Ancestors Back from the Grave." Frank Perdue's tag line "It takes a tough man to make a tender chicken," when translated into Spanish actually means "It takes a sexually stimulated man to make a chicken affectionate." For my personal favorite, Gerber®, with quite a bit of public embarrassment, had to quickly discontinue its then current marketing approach in Africa. It is the custom in Africa to show a picture of what is inside the jar on the label because of the inability of many people there to read, and what does the typical jar of Gerber's® baby food show on the label? A smiling baby.

Camps will make mistakes with diverse populations, but the root cause of most mistakes is a lack of forethought regarding diversity management. We might well be able to swell our camp ranks with nontraditional populations, but if they have a less than positive experience we have negated all of our recruitment efforts. One residential camp director was highly desirous of including Laotian children in her program. The local communities had seen a great increase in the number of such families in the previous decade. After much effort, a small number of children were enrolled for one encampment. The well-intentioned director had been proactive enough to consider language barriers but had not considered food preferences, hygiene practices, social interactions with other campers, and general desire for parental involvement. In the end, these children had a less than positive experience, and unfortunately the camp director has been unable to attract the attention of any other Laotian families since the occurrence.

It is the management of diversity that will be the proverbial "thorn in the side" for many camp administrators. We will have to begin by recognizing that many of our assumptions and values cannot be generalized to other populations and that successful management of diversity will require changes in human-resources management, child-management practices, and camp activities. If we naively assume that diverse populations will come to our camps and simply assimilate our pre-existing practices, we are headed for failure. Assimilation as defined by Ward, Bochner, and Furnham (2001) "refers to the process whereby a group or a whole society gradually adopt, or are forced into adopting, the customs, values, lifestyles, and language of a more dominate culture." (p. 29) Instead, we must begin to explore the changes that the camp industry will have to make in order to manage diversity. Notice that the sentence does not read "changes that diverse populations will have to make to fit into our camps." We are the ones required to change.

I began this article with a discussion of cognitive maps and their advantages and disadvantages. The major disadvantage of cognitive maps is that they can entrap us into one way of perceiving and acting in the world. It is already evident that diversity issues are affecting camps and that the future of our industry hinges on our ability to work with diverse populations. Therefore, I ask readers to please introspect on their own model of diversity. If the model is one of adding nontraditional populations without considering changes that camps must make, success will not occur. Again, our camps, and ultimately ourselves, must change (and some changes will be dramatic and uncomfortable) for true successful diversity to occur.

References

Halter, M. (2000). *Shopping for Identity: The Marketing of Ethnicity*. New York: Schocken Books.

McGehee, T. (2001). *Whoosh*. Massachusetts: Perseus Publishing.

McKibben, B. (2006). Year One: Climate chaos has arrived. *Sierra*, 91(1), 30-35.

Smith, P. (2004). "Promoting Diversity Through Innovative Programs". *Camping Magazine*, July/August, 14-15.

Ward, C., Bochner, S., & Furnham, A. (2001). *The Psychology of Culture Shock.* Pennsylvania: Routledge.

15

Staff Sexual Assault—Prevention and Intervention

by Michael Shelton, M.S., C.A.C., C.F.T.

It's 10:30 at night, and you're tired. The campers have been in their bunks for a little less than an hour. The staff is thankfully quiet. All in all, it has been a good day. Just before you leave the camp office, two figures approach. One is your girls' program director; she has her arm wrapped over the shoulder of a female counselor. You can tell that the counselor has been crying.

"We need to talk," the program director tells you. You can tell by the tone in her voice that this is serious. She gently pats the counselor on the shoulder as a sign that she should begin. The counselor looks down at the floor. Her voice is so low that you can barely hear her words. "Mark (a counselor in boys' camp) tried to rape me."

What do you do?

Sexual assault is an inclusive label that subsumes many sexual acts. These typically include forced sexual contact (e.g., fondling, kissing, and petting), attempted rape, and completed rape. The common factor is that a person is touched in an unwelcome sexual way. Many camp directors, when faced with an accusation of sexual assault, respond in one of two contrasting ways. In the first, the camp director simply fires the accused. The risk here is that the accused is innocent of the charges. In the second, the response is to minimize the dilemma. The accused might be told to not do it again and then put back into the camp community—the consequence is merely a proverbial "slap on the wrist."

Both responses affect the entire camp community. Because of the intimacy inherent in a camp environment, news of a sexual assault is bound to spread. An immediate termination risks a reputation of unfairness for the director. The marginal punishment, on the other hand, is evidence to staff that the camp director does not take the issue of safety seriously. If one staff member can sexually attack another member without repercussions, what else will staff members get away with? Of course, in particularly egregious cases, an immediate termination along with police involvement is a necessity. In others, a minimal response is sufficient. Many camp directors unfortunately have a tendency to rely on one of these two responses. However, each case of sexual assault is different; no one solution will work in every case. Camp directors need the appropriate information that allows them to respond in a reasonable, efficient, timely, and defendable manner in incidents of sexual assault between staff members.

Sexual Assaults in Camps

The American Camp Association's *The CampLine* presents an annual account of calls to the ACA hotline for camp-related problems. For the summer of 2002, there were three allegations of staff-on-staff sexual abuse (Scanlin, 2002). The 2003 edition reported no such allegations. The overwhelming majority of incidents of sexual assault that occur in the United States is never reported. Camps that experience such behaviors may have purposely refrained from reporting the incidents. Another more likely reason for the lack of reporting is simply because these occurrences did not come to the attention of camp administrators.

While a sexual assault by a stranger may occur on camp property, we have a much more realistic concern with such violence occurring within a relationship. In fact, most cases of sexual assault take place within the confines of a pre-established relationship. These relationships can be between friends, romantic partners, or just a passing acquaintanceship. Rarely do they occur between individuals who had no prior contact. In most cases of forced sexual activity, we are referring to a victim as a female and a perpetrator as a male. Because of the size difference between males and females, females are the common victims in reported sexual-assault cases. It is difficult for a female to be intimidating to a male if she is smaller, weighs less, and is not as strong.

A Developmental Perspective on Sexual Assault

It is difficult to be partial when a victim of sexual assault is describing an attack. One will naturally be inclined to have sympathy for the victim and disdain for the accused. While it might be tempting to slip into polarized thinking at this point with an easily identified victim and villain, the reality is that such thinking may be more harmful than helpful for all involved parties.

It is likely that the cause of a sexual assault between staff members in camp is that a male misinterpreted a female's cues concerning sexual activity. There are three underlying reasons for such an occurrence. First, males and females do not typically enter romantic relationships with the same set of interpersonal skills. As the result of often vastly different experiences in childhood, romantic relationships are frequently tumultuous. Research has found:

- Between the ages of three and four, children increasingly prefer to play with same-sex children until the early teenage years.

- The play style between the same-sex groupings is quite different: males prefer active play with displays of dominance while females prefer more cooperative and interpersonal interactions (Collins, Hennighausen, Schmit, and Sroufe, 1997).

Because of such segregation, boys and girls grow up with different experiences of the world and learn different interpersonal skills. These different skill sets assure that there will be misunderstandings and complications when the two sexes interact. This often vast difference in interpersonal skills is particularly complicated when it comes to sexual interactions.

The second underlying reason is that in many cases there is no direct request for sexual activity—much of the initiation of sexual activity between two people occurs through indirect means. Males may treat a date to a very expensive meal, attempt to ingratiate themselves, and profess love to partners that they in no way actually feel. A study by Greer and Buss (1994) found that the most successful tactic to engage a female in sexual activity is to invest time and attention as well as profess love and commitment. In regards to females, Perper and Weis (1987) found that females also have an armory of techniques to express sexual interest including talking (e.g., laughing, complimenting, sexual talk), environmental signaling (e.g., seductive clothing, dancing, creating a "romantic atmosphere"), touching (e.g., holding hands, caressing), and kissing.

While it would certainly be easier to directly ask a person for their interest in participation in sexual activity, the reality is that many couples rely on less-direct methods. It is the ambiguity of the indirect methods that is often the root cause of a sexual assault that occurs in camp. Males in particular tend to misinterpret even the most neutral signals as sexual invitations. Likewise, males often misinterpret a female's protestations as mere token resistance; in some males' eyes, a woman's statement of "no" is a façade in effect so as not to appear too sexually available.

There is one final additional complication to the already complex mix of interpersonal skills, differences between the sexes, and the ambiguities of sexual signaling and interpretation—sexual arousal affects the functioning of the human brain.

Sexual arousal can interfere with judgment and self-control. Such arousal may not only lower one's inhibitions and lead to the use of coercion but additionally reduces awareness of the reactions of one's partner. Long-term consequences are minimized or out-and-out ignored during moments of passion.

In summary, when a staff member reports a sexual assault, it is highly unlikely that the alleged perpetrator is a sexual psychopath. A more realistic appraisal is that a male may have misinterpreted mutual sexual interest on the part of a female. However, this does not excuse his behavior.

Prevention and Intervention

A director is legally obligated by federal law to intervene to stop sexual harassment in a camp. An isolated sexual assault on a co-worker would likely not be classified as sexual harassment as it is delineated in the regulations of the Equal Employment Opportunity Commission (EEOC), the federal agency established to deal with workplace discrimination. An assault committed by a supervisor, however, is always sexual harassment. In the case of camps, I recommend that all camps take a sexual harassment-prevention perspective even when the assault occurs between co-workers. It offers not only a recognized legal model for intervention but also makes practical sense in coping with the aftereffects of an accusation. A singular incident of unwanted physical contact may indicate an environmental problem with a camp. Maybe it is less safe than the director believes. Maybe there are numerous unwanted sexual behaviors occurring that remain hidden from the administration. This supposedly isolated incident may reveal troubling undercurrents.

The following are several guidelines for a camp director to keep in mind when a sexual assault is reported.

1. Stay calm.

It does not help anybody if the camp director loses control in a critical incident. Many directors will be worried about the implications of such an incident on their own and their camps' reputations instead of focusing on more important immediate action steps. For example, I can recall quite well the first time I had to intervene in a sexual assault incident in a camp. Not only was I concerned with the welfare of the participants involved but also the reputation of the camp as well as my own. How should I handle this event? Had I somehow allowed this to incident to inadvertently occur? How would this incident reflect on my leadership? Would I lose my job over the occurrence? Would the media somehow become involved? Such concerns prevented my full attention to the immediate incident.

2. Give the victim partial control of the situation.

A sexual assault is a crime no matter what degree of seriousness it entails. The most important choice a victim can make is whether she wants to call the police or not. This contact initiates involvement of the legal system, and it is this system that will determine whether a crime has occurred. It is not the victim's choice however to determine the punishment of the offender (e.g., Should he be fired?). I have heard of camps that granted this right to a victim. Remember, an accusation against a person does not necessarily equate with actual guilt.

Some aspects need to be considered in regards to police investigation. First, every state now has a mandatory-reporting protocol in place for child abuse. If the victimized staff member is under the age of 18, the director may be obligated to report this to a youth-protective agency. Second, some camps have a policy that requires police to question all cases of sexual assault even if the victim declines such involvement; this is done not so much for the protection of the victim but rather to have a written record on file for the camp's own legal security. The downside to mandating police investigation is that it might deter a female from reporting less severe incidents to the administration if she knows that she will have to speak to police. It is recommended that all directors contact their local police and youth-protective agency to ascertain their requirements for incidents of sexual assault.

3. The camp director is not a judge.

The good news is that camp directors are not responsible to decide innocence or guilt. This is a decision that the legal system undertakes. For camp directors to attempt to secure evidence that reaches the standard of "beyond a reasonable doubt" as is used in the criminal courts is ill advised, no matter how well intentioned. The duty of the director is to create a safe environment and make all efforts to prevent similar assaults. The legal obligation of all employers is to establish and maintain a workplace free of harassment. This is a vastly different duty as compared to ascertaining guilt or innocence.

A problem that naturally arises in situations of sexual assault is how to respond to the accused. How can a director act on an accusation of assault if he or she is not making a determination of guilt or innocence? Some assaults are particularly violent and/or occur in the presence of witnesses. Such physical harm of another camp participant is undoubtedly against your camp policy—this behavior is grounds for immediate termination even if the victim in the case declines police involvement. Most occurrences of assault that occur in camp though will be less obvious. Instead of a female presenting bruises and torn clothing, a more common case will present no evidence of physical harm. For example, a male and female staff member go to a bar on their night off and then return slightly intoxicated; the male in question begins to make sexual advances upon the female including groping her and using obscene language. She quickly leaves and reports the incident to her immediate supervisor.

The crux of the dilemma is how one is to weigh the welfare of the victim and ramifications for the camp's reputation against a wrongful termination. It is here that an investigation by the director will occur with the sole purpose of collecting information that will lead to creating a harassment-free environment. If the male in question is too much of a risk to the camp environment for future harassment, a decision to terminate may be made. Variables such as frequency of the act, severity of the act, and intentionally intended harm versus unintentional interactions all play a role in the decision to terminate, discipline, or do nothing. Incidentally, the victim in an incident does not have to be completely satisfied with the outcome of an investigation. If she seeks a decision of guilt and resulting punishment, this is the responsibility of the legal system. A camp director instead must be reasonable and effective in dealing with the alleged sexual assault. A decision on how successful a camp director is in his or her response to an accusation of assault is based on the reasonableness, effectiveness, and expediency of the investigation and intervention, not the complete satisfaction of the victim with the consequences for the offender. It certainly helps the process though if the victim is kept informed of the investigation and given an opportunity to offer an opinion on whether a proposed intervention will work.

A successful intervention simply needs to be one that stops future unwanted behaviors. An assault intervention can be approached as would most interpersonal problems at camp including remedies such as problem solving, education, consciousness-raising, and boundary setting. For the latter in particular, keep in mind that it has only been in the past 50 years that males and females have worked together. Males and females are still attempting to learn each other's boundaries. Sadly, society has offered few positive role models for males on respecting female boundaries.

4. Find legal counsel.

Each camp should have a legal representative. Refer questions to this person. Do not attempt to resolve these issues completely on your own. You want to be certain that a well-meaning intervention does not later turn into a legal problem. As more and more sexual harassment disputes are heard in the court, the laws for this area will become more refined. A director most certainly does not want to have his camp branded with a sexual harassment lawsuit.

The Best Intervention Is Prevention

The best intervention for sexual assault (as well as all harmful sexual activity) is prevention. A camp's response to a sexual assault should come as no surprise to camp staff. It is assumed that at this point all camps have formulated a sexual-harassment policy that will specifically mention unwanted physical contact. In addition, staff should be informed in writing and during a staff-week orientation what specific procedure will occur if a sexual assault is reported. They should know the camp's stance on refusing to determine guilt, police involvement, and possible consequences. They should also know that the obligation of the director in such a case is to implement changes that would lead to a safer and harassment-free environment. This might or might not entail punishment for the offender, dependent on the details of the incident.

Another significant step to decrease the chances of a sexual assault is to monitor the use of alcohol. A significant minority of sexual assaults occurs while one or both parties are under the influence of alcohol. The ever-increasing use of random alcohol screening with invariant consequences for its use will go a long way in deterring such assaults.

Even with the best prevention plan, incidents will happen. Instead of reliance on the common responses of immediate termination of the accused or minimal intervention in the incident, the director should undertake an investigation with the ultimate goal of increasing camp safety for all participants. In the unlikely situation of an extremely violent assault, it is reassuring to know that the camp director does not need to have all of the answers.

References

Buss, D. (2000). *The Dangerous Passion*. New York: The Free Press.

Buss, D. (2003). *The Evolution of Desire*. New York: Basic Books.

Collins, W.A., Hennighausen, K., Schmit, D., & Sroufe, L.A. (1997). Developmental precursors of romantic relationships: A longitudinal perspective. In S. Shulman & W.A.

Collins (Eds.), *Romantic Relationships in Adolescence: Developmental Perspectives* (pp. 69-84). California: Jossey–Bass Publishers.

Greer, A.E., & Buss, D. M. (1994). "Tactics for Promoting Sexual Encounters". *Journal of Sex Research*, 31, 185-201.

Perper, T., & Weis, D. (1987). "Proceptive and Rejective Strategies of U.S. and Canadian College Women". *Journal of Sex Research*, 23, 455-480.

Rutter, P. (1996). *Sex, Power, and Boundaries*. New York: Bantam.

Scanlin, M. (2002). "Summary of 2002 ACA Hotline Calls". *The CampLine*, 2, 1 & 8-9.

Scanlin, M (2003). "Summary of ACA Hotline Calls". *The CampLine*, 2, 1 & 8-9.

Wagner, E. (1992). *Sexual Harassment in the Workplace*. New York: Amacom.

16

Seven Habits of Highly Effective Camps

by Christopher A. Thurber, Ph.D.

Rebuild or Reload?

Highly effective camps establish more than a healthy culture. They incorporate habits that keep the camping fundamentals solid and that afford them the luxury of fine-tuning the delivery of their stated mission. Such camps can elevate a simple kickball game into a classroom for teamwork and sportsmanship—without the campers ever knowing. They can nurture the strengths that individual campers and cabin leaders possess, thus increasing the likelihood they will return the following season. Because highly effective camps are not overwhelmed with struggling to meet their basic needs, they can fine-tune their responses to feedback from campers, staff, and parents, thus setting themselves on a course of perpetual self-improvement. In summary, these camps do not rebuild each season—they reload.

Seven Habits and Their Benefits

Good camps have an explicit and thoughtful mission statement. Great camps succeed at actually delivering that mission. In my experience, such highly effective camps share seven habits that are essential elements of success.

1. Internal leadership development

2. Explicit expectations for staff

3. Ample camper preparation

4. Personal relationships

5. Supervisors-in-residence

6. Bi-directional communication flow

7. Commitment to self-improvement

Incorporating these habits has three key outcomes for directors, staff, front-line cabin leaders, and campers:

- deep satisfaction;

- enriched learning; and

- increased tenure.

If asked, "Will you come back?" on closing day, children and employees at highly effective camps relate simple and beautiful words that go something like this—"I love this place; I learned a lot; and I'll be back next year." All three key outcomes are there—satisfaction, learning, and tenure.

Practicing these seven habits is a prodigious task that requires energy, vigilance, and patience. "No rest for the weary" is the rule of thumb at highly effective camps, but to those who have seen the benefits of their labor, no work could be more gratifying. The sections that follow describe the seven habits seen at highly effective camps, the benefits of their practice, and an action plan for adopting each one.

Internal leadership development

Internal leadership development (ILD) is a process of promoting and training your own campers to become junior leaders, leaders-in-training, and eventually full-fledged cabin leaders and senior staff. (See *Camping Magazine*, Vol. 74, November/December 2001, pp. 24-29 for detailed guidelines on designing an ILD system that works for your camp.) Having an ILD system at your camp means first having a clear idea of the qualities you seek in cabin leaders—such as enthusiasm, unselfishness, initiative, integrity, and a love of camp. You must then have a process of selecting, from among the ranks of your oldest campers, those who demonstrate trainable leadership qualities. Over the next two or three seasons of experiential learning, these young men and women will become your next generation of cabin leaders. ILD systems work best under the direction of experienced senior staff who can mentor and evaluate up-and-coming leaders. Some camps even have a designated leadership director, whose primary job is to coordinate the ILD system. New ILD systems take about five years to bear fruit and about ten years to perfect.

The benefits of ILD are manifold, but the best part is that your cabin leaders, those who deal most directly with your campers, have not a week of training, but two summers' worth. There is truly no comparison between a first-time hire with no previous camp experience and someone who has grown up in your camp and then been mentored for two summers. Both will participate in staff training week, but your new hires will know roughly 10 percent of what they need to do their job well. By contrast, your homegrown leaders already understand and live the camp's culture, know your policies and schedule logistics like the back of their hands, and have infinitely more experience working with your camper population.

What does that mean for you, the director? It means that during staff-training week, you can fine-tune. You can focus on advanced leadership techniques, review the mistakes made in the previous season, and solidify bonds of friendship. Little of this precious time will be spent teaching camp songs, explaining the daily schedule, or praying that all those new hires will obey the rules and not quit before mid-season. Although painstaking to establish, ILD saves you time in the long run, provides multi-year training, and gives you peace of mind.

Explicit expectations

All of your employees, from the freshest junior leader to the most seasoned senior staff, will be better prepared to do their jobs when you've taken time to make your expectations explicit. This means spelling out, in great detail, each person's job description. Don't assume they know what you want, and don't assume they will read lengthy written material. Clearly tell them, in face-to-face meetings, what you expect from them, what specifically is forbidden, and what the consequences are of breaking major rules.

If most of your staff are former campers, stating explicit expectations is a straight-forward task. For external hires, you must be especially careful, in both interviews and on-site training, to make your expectations explicit. If you'll be asking your archery program head to help lifeguard, be sure she knows that ahead of time. If you allot your staff one weeknight off per week, make that clear, so they're not disappointed on Saturday night. Also be sure you accurately describe your camp to prospective hires in all interviews you conduct. Describe your camp's culture, traditions, daily schedule, spiritual and religious customs, work ethic, time-off policies, pay scale, and grounds for termination.

The central benefit of stating expectations explicitly is that you'll never hear complaints that begin with "No one ever told me I had to..." Most disgruntled staff would have been happy to do what their directors requested if they knew about it when they were hired. Disgruntled staff, of course, foment discontent among all but the most resilient and devoted staff. In so doing, they destroy morale.

Camper preparation

Campers, especially first-year campers, need coaching on how to get the most out of your camp. For starters, they need to know what to bring (and what not to bring); how to prevent severe homesickness; which behaviors are encouraged and which are unacceptable; and what is included in the daily schedule. Campers' parents also need lots of coaching on what to do with their own anxiety. Each summer, thousands of campers struggle with severe homesickness because their parents have made "pick-up deals" with them. Parents promise, "If you feel homesick, I'll come and get you." Such well-intentioned but ignorant remarks sabotage a child's confidence and dramatically increase the likelihood that such a child will become severely homesick.

The benefits of proper camper preparation include both reduced homesickness and better camper behavior overall. Moreover, families with adequate preparation, those who have "bought in" to your camp's rules, regulations, and behavioral standards, are far less likely to bring contraband to camp, argue with your discipline system, or complain about your policies. Providing ample camper preparation is the cornerstone of partnering with parents.

Personal relationships

Management experts and camp consultants alike emphasize the importance of directors establishing an authoritative leadership relationship with their staff. Cabin leaders are also urged to establish this type of relationship with their campers. Unfortunately, what sometimes occurs out of a misguided attempt to keep "professional distance" is that directors and senior staff fail to develop personal relationships with their front-line cabin leaders, or cabin leaders fail to develop a personal relationship with their campers. The solution? Directors and senior staff must learn each cabin leader's name, know something about each one, and touch base with each one during the course of the summer to convey what is being done well and what needs improvement. For their part, cabin leaders must learn their campers' names, know what they like and dislike, empathize with their emotional experiences, and guide them.

Some personal attention must also be paid to camper families, especially in pre-season. If you have a couple hundred camper families, you can actually get to know something about each one. If you have more, then your personal touch might come in the form of a signed holiday letter, photos posted on your camp's website, or a camp news bulletin sent to each family.

Loyalty is the key benefit of establishing personal relationships with staff, campers, and camper families. Establishing personal relationships pays dividends simply because people enjoy recognition. They want you to know their name, something about their personal history, and something about what they do at camp. Only then will they be willing to respond to feedback. Staff and campers also want genuine, specific praise. Delivering this will make staff want to work twice as hard for you and will boost camper return rates.

Supervisors-in-residence

When cabin leaders feel that their direct supervisors are out of touch with camper demographics, cabin dynamics, and specific camper issues, they become frustrated. Who wants to take orders or advice from supervisors who don't live what they teach? Of course, every camp has some out-of-cabin senior staff positions—such as your program director. That's a good thing, given the responsibilities and schedules of these folks, but what highly effective camps also have are some unit leaders or division heads who live in cabins with campers. In the camp's management structure, these are essential players because they see, first-hand, what goes on. They are therefore in the best position to mentor younger cabin leaders and update the director about emerging problems.

There are several obvious benefits to having key leaders living in cabins. They know what's really going on in your camp, which makes them seem approachable to your cabin leaders. Cabin leaders are also more willing to listen to feedback from someone who walks the walk. Best of all, having key leaders live in cabins helps nip most leadership and camper behavior problems in the bud before they become large enough to demand your precious time.

Bi-directional communication flow

Communication happens at all camps, including camps that struggle to deliver their mission. What makes a highly effective camp stand out is bi-directional communication flow—messages and feedback travel smoothly up and down the management tree. At all camps, employees at the bottom of the hierarchy receive messages from above. At highly effective camps, messages are also sent in the other direction, so that directors and senior staff receive frequent reports from the front lines.

This is not to say that the upper management of camp needs to be informed every time a camper burps, but they should know about such things as severe homesickness, enuresis, and aggression. The benefits of bi-directional communication flow are similar to those of having supervisors-in-residence, with two added benefits. First, armed with accurate information about noteworthy campers, directors are in a better position to handle phone calls from anxious parents. Second, directors can be assured that the information they share with division heads and unit leaders gets disseminated. Few things make cabin leaders feel less important than finding out details of important camp events at the last minute, worse yet, finding out from their campers. At highly effective camps, every employee feels both responsible (they are entrusted with information) and responsive (they entrust others with information).

Commitment to self-improvement

A genuine commitment to perpetual self-improvement dovetails with the preceding six habits and is the lifeblood of highly effective camps. Establishing or enhancing your internal leadership development, explicit expectations, camper preparation, personal relationships, supervisors-in-residence, and bi-directional communication flow will require careful self-examination. Living each of these habits demands that you and your staff decide what your camp is meant to do. If you are a force for change in the universe, what do you seek to change and how? If you represent certain values, what vehicles do you use to communicate those values and how do you measure their effects?

No source of information is more valuable than empirical data. Gut feelings and anecdotes have tremendous value, but are less reliable than information derived from the scheduled administration of well-designed questionnaires or from structured feedback sessions. You need not conduct major research at your camp each season, but it is worthwhile to gather data regularly from campers, parents, and staff in a way that tells you whether you are actually delivering your stated mission. Humility is only half of the self-improvement equation. You must also gather hard data to see where you may be falling short of your stated goals. Many camp consultants offer research services and can provide objective feedback on your camp's strengths, as well as ideas for remedying weaknesses.

Besides professional consultation, other essential sources of data include: regularly scheduled full-staff meetings, ACA standards visitors, state inspectors, and structured reports from all levels of your leadership. Finally, to disseminate what you learn from all these data, it's imperative to learn and teach how to give and receive feedback. Many camps falter not at the data-gathering phase of self-improvement, but at the implementation phase.

Mission-Driven or Market-Driven?

These seven habits of highly effective camps are certainly practical, in the sense of being useful and realistic, but only to a mission-driven camp. Are you mission-driven or market-driven?

For mission-driven camps, the ends justify the means. For example, if part of such a camp's mission is to instill a sense of personal responsibility in its campers, the cabin leaders and campers might clean the cabin each morning and complete camp duties each day. If parents and campers complain "we didn't pay good money to clean like slaves each day," a mission-driven camp will politely suggest the names of other camps, but will not succumb to such complaints. If such a camp sticks to its principles, all the bunks will eventually be filled with children whose parents respect the notion that a sense of personal responsibility is earned through hard work and accountability. Ultimately, a mission-driven camp's integrity pays dividends. Bunks are full and children are absorbing the camp's mission.

By contrast, a market-driven camp will adjust the means, even if it entails compromising the ends. For example, a market-driven camp might respond to parent and camper complaints of "slave labor" by making the cabin leaders clean the cabins alone or by hiring a custodial staff to perform camp duties. Market-driven camps seek to please their customers without educating them. They are more concerned with giving campers what they want than giving them what they need to absorb the camp's mission.

As you strive to make your camp even more effective, examine the ways in which you are mission-driven and market-driven. The more mission-driven you are, the more easily you will adopt these seven habits. In addition, the more you adopt these seven habits, the more campers will take home your mission.

17

More Than a Village—Fostering a Community Response to Underage Drinking

by Stephen G. Wallace, M.S. Ed.

Anyone who has attended or worked at a summer camp knows the experience transcends that offered by the mere existence of soccer balls, tennis courts, or sailboats. Camps are communities—villages really, and at their best maybe more.

Folklore, common sense, and even recent research on resiliency suggest that children thrive best in environments rich with structure, supervision, and the guidance of caring adults. Like neighborhoods of yesteryear, summer camps foster a collective responsibility to and accountability for all the children, not just those living in a particular cabin or learning a certain skill.

Building on the nuclear family, camp counselors pick up where parents leave off— nurturing healthy exploration, achievement, self-reliance, and respect for oneself, for others, and for the community at large. Many of these same tenets have found their way into the prevention principles that ground important efforts to keep youth alcohol-free, suggesting a mutuality of interest and impact between camp programs and those designed to keep young people, particularly teens, safe and alive. Indeed, camps can play a pivotal role in reinforcing and even establishing expectations regarding the advisability and acceptability of underage drinking.

Why Bother?

A report from the National Research Council and the Institute of Medicine of the National Academies (Reducing Underage Drinking: A Collective Responsibility) sounds the alarm on an epidemic of youth and alcohol. So, too, does *Teens Today* research from SADD and Liberty Mutual Group:

- Drinking increases significantly between the sixth and seventh grades.
- The average age for teens to start drinking is thirteen years old.
- By twelfth grade, more than three in four teens are drinking.

Unfortunately, many young people fall prey to the Myth of Invincibility, believing that there are no real or lasting effects of alcohol use. They're wrong:

- The younger a child is when he or she starts to drink, the higher the chances he or she will have alcohol-related problems later in life.
- Alcohol use by teens affects still-developing cognitive abilities and impairs memory and learning.
- Teens that drink are more likely to commit or be the victim of violence (including sexual assault) and to experience depression and suicidal thoughts.
- Alcohol-related automobile crashes kill thousands of teens each year and injure millions more.

In turn, many of the important adults in teens' lives may also subscribe to the Myth of Inevitability—convinced that drinking is a rite of passage for youth and that there's not much they can do to influence a young person's choices. They're wrong, too:

- More than a third of middle and high school students say they have not consumed alcohol.
- Adults who talk with teens about underage drinking, set expectations, and enforce consequences can discourage experimentation with alcohol. (This influence holds true for other teen behaviors such as drug use and early sexual activity.)
- Young people say they want guidance in making decisions about personal behavior, including alcohol use.

Although alcohol consumption is often perceived as less of a concern among anti-drug efforts, underage drinking clearly remains a substantial threat. Indeed, the National Academies' report estimates the annual cost to be $53 billion in losses from traffic deaths, violent crime, and other destructive behavior, to say nothing of the damage to mental health, school performance, and relationships with parents and peers. It is past time to reconcile the forces of indifference and indulgence that perpetuate underage drinking with the urgent need to protect children.

The report calls for a series of steps it suggests will change the face of "normative" behavior when it comes to adolescents and alcohol. In the spirit of "it takes a village," it also serves up a strategy suggesting the participation of almost all segments of society. With the camp industry's extraordinary capacity to "reach" youth, summer camps should be no exception.

Perhaps most significant, the report suggests an array of youth-oriented interventions aimed not only at increasing self-esteem or decreasing peer pressure, but also at activities that educate, intervene, and enforce. However, making those efforts effective requires a close examination of the factors that influence young people to drink in the first place.

Not surprisingly, some teens say they drink to have fun, fit in, or just to do what their friends seem to be doing, but engaging in destructive behaviors is not just about "having a good time." Many teens, particularly older ones, drink to escape problems. Left unaddressed, those problems can pose a significant risk to healthy social and emotional development. So, too, does a lack of experience in solving them.

The data also indicates other key drivers of decisions about alcohol, including depression, anxiety, stress, and boredom; a desire to feel grown up and to take risks; a fear of getting caught; and the influence of parents, friends, and siblings. So what does this tell us? That there are practical approaches camp counselors can take to reduce the likelihood that young people will turn to alcohol.

- Monitor campers' emotional health and intervene at signs of trouble. Anxiety, and its close cousin depression, correlates highly with alcohol use. So does boredom—so find things for teens to do that both stimulate and challenge.

- Help teens achieve their goals. They want to be successful, to grow up, and to take risks. Channel that risk-taking tendency toward activities that enhance healthy socialization with peers and positive feelings about themselves. Also, take time to point out ways in which alcohol use can interfere with success in academics and athletics.

- Establish (and enforce) consequences for bad behavior. Young people need clear boundaries and appreciate adults who care enough to patrol them.

- Be a good role model. Not surprisingly, Teens Today research revealed that students in grades 6-12 report that those they are close to are most influential in their decisions not to drink.

Most importantly: communicate. Young people who have caring adults willing to take the time to talk with them about underage drinking benefit from hearing about the risks associated with alcohol use and strategies to avoid it.

Unfortunately, too many influential role models send too many messages that encourage or enable underage drinking, while many others simply expect or ignore it. Agreeing to disagree about this important issue obscures an alarming indifference about youth and alcohol, but it does nothing to keep teens safe and alive. Not until society speaks with one, clear, unambiguous voice about the perils of underage drinking, as the National Academies' report suggests, will it successfully shatter the myths of invincibility and inevitability that propel it.

Our highways and hospitals are lined with young people who made poor, even fatal, choices about alcohol. Still many more suffer silently, unable to meet their own life goals or to realize the promise their friends, parents, and other caring adults see in them. Understanding teen drinking readies deployment of the many people needed to prevent it, including camp counselors. As the ancient African proverb teaches, it will take a village. Maybe more.

18

Their Space or Yours—Social Networking Sites Bring Risks and Rewards to the Camp Community

by Stephen G. Wallace, M.S.Ed

The popularity of social networking sites, such as Myspace.com, Facebook.com, Xanga.com, and Friendster.com, raise new and important issues for camp directors intent on protecting their campers and their camps from the dark side of the online world. The recent explosion in membership to such sites (MySpace, for example, grew from zero to 47.3 million members in just two years) only increases the urgency of addressing online behavior and its potential risks and rewards for the camp community.

On these high-tech versions of the "local" hangout, young people post personal information often accompanied by pictures of themselves and their friends. Cloaked in a false sense of anonymity, they too often abandon good judgment, even common sense, by providing intimate details about their lives for all the world to see, including home and email addresses, cell-phone numbers, or details about body type, sexual preferences, or alcoholic beverages of choice. The information flow doesn't stop there. A *Dateline NBC* investigation of teen pages found scenes of binge drinking, apparent drug use, and sex acts.

Concerns About Youth Safety

Law-enforcement officials are so concerned that at least two states, Connecticut and Massachusetts, are investigating the link between these sites and incidents of sexual assault, but they're not going it alone. The Federal Bureau of Investigation (FBI) says that it has opened dozens of cases nationwide regarding activity on the sites and has received more than 500 complaints, including the following.

- Earlier this year, a 33-year old Alabama man met a 14-year old girl from New Jersey over one site and later abused her in Florida.
- In October 2005, a 13-year old girl from Georgia, whose online profile said she was 29, was abused by a 30-year old South Carolina man.
- Last September, an 11-year old girl was fondled in her Connecticut home, while her parents slept, by a man she'd met through an online network and let into her home.

Such cases are likely the proverbial "tip of the iceberg," prompting a cascade of overdue media attention.

L.J. Ulrich, a student columnist at West Virginia University, checked out MySpace and reported, "I signed on, created my generic profile, and reached out. Then the freaks reached out to me. It's like standing in the kitchen naked and leaving the front door wide open. Anybody can stalk anybody, and anybody can play games. Until it adopts some restrictions, MySpace is just another haven for the freaks of the Internet and naïve 10-year olds."

Those restrictions may not be far behind. While MySpace itself recently beefed up security on its site, others are jumping into the fray. In Massachusetts, for example, Attorney General Tom Reilly called upon MySpace to put in place strict controls to protect children. "MySpace allows 14- and 15-year olds to register as members of its 'community' and claims to be able to protect their safety," Reilly said. "Our investigation revealed that these measures are not effective and do not protect children from being exposed to inappropriate content they just shouldn't see." He then called on MySpace to improve the safety and security of its site by:

- Instituting an age and identity verification system;
- Equipping every MySpace page with a "Report Inappropriate Content" link;
- Responding to all reports of inappropriate content within 24 hours;
- Increasing significantly the number of employees who review images and content on the MySpace website;
- Implementing filtering technology that effectively blocks sexually explicit or violent images;
- Immediately deleting any profiles that violate MySpace's Terms of Use Agreement and permanently banning those members from using the site;
- Immediately removing all advertisements and other MySpace-sponsored content that are inappropriate for children; and
- Offering free, downloadable software that allows parents to block use of MySpace.

Child predators and inappropriate content aren't the only problems, and harm to youth not the only risk. A review of Myspace.com reveals "group" pages created by children and teens and incorporating the name, and sometimes the logo, of their school or camp. These virtual campfires allow for cyberbullying toward camps, campers, and staff and the unsupervised exchange of often-inappropriate ideas and pictures that would never be tolerated within the confines of a classroom or cabin. One camp counselor found some of the online profiles of her campers "disturbing." Parents, who in some cases are mercilessly maligned in their child's answers to online questionnaires, have been similarly dismayed.

In some instances, the content amounts to sexual innuendo and in others not-so-subtle sexual solicitation. Also featured are photos of kissing, fondling, and groping (one such site featured a photograph of a penis) and dialogue about getting high, getting wasted, or just plain getting mad. All of this under the banner of organizations committed to education, youth development, and safety.

A natural reaction might be to simply ban teen participation in online networking, but attempting to deny campers' access may ultimately fail, for they would likely just migrate to other online venues. Besides, social networking sites do have useful purposes, both in terms of youth development and in extending the benefits of summer camp beyond the front gate.

Social Networking Sites and Youth Development

As camp professionals, we are committed to the principles of youth development and the outcomes directly related to what we do. As revealed in *Directions, Youth Development Outcomes of the Camp Experience*, a study conducted by Philliber Research Associates and the American Camp Association, these include increased self-esteem, independence, leadership, friendship skills, and social comfort. Just as there is a link between camp and healthy development, so too may there be a positive role for social networking sites.

As children mature, and particularly during their teenage years, they are charged with three important developmental tasks.

1. Attaining a stable sense of personal identity

2. Becoming more independent from their parents

3. Establishing meaningful and fulfilling relationships with their peers

Each is an important building block toward becoming a happy, healthy, and productive adult. A recent *Teens Today* study from SADD (Students Against Destructive Decisions) and Liberty Mutual Group, established a clear link between a young person's progress in these key areas with their overall sense of self. Young people who perceive they are doing well in addressing such issues are more likely than those who don't to feel smart, successful, responsible, and confident.

In many ways, social networking sites facilitate the very type of independence and exploration that allows young people to try on different roles (or personas) and to gather feedback from their all-important, and arguably more objective, peer group. They may also help campers make new friends. One 16-year old camp veteran did so "using MySpace for what it was intended."

Extending Camp Beyond the Front Gate

Social networking sites also provide potential benefits to camps, facilitating year-round connections between campers once largely separated by the unlikely, and burdensome, exercise of keeping in touch through Ma Bell or the U.S. Postal Service. One camper who organized a group site on MySpace explained, "I saw that a lot of people from camp already had accounts and thought it was a good way to connect everybody and keep in touch." That is an important perspective for camp leaders interested in nurturing throughout the year the positive relationships developed during the summer. There are, however, other important steps we should take to keep our campers and our camps safe.

Keeping Campers and Camps Safe

First, it is important to educate campers about the risks associated with online activity and to suggest concrete ways to stay safe. i-SAFE America, www.isafe.org, a nonprofit foundation dedicated to Internet safety education for youth, outlines "The 4 Rs" of Internet safety.

- Recognize techniques used by online predators to deceive.
- Refuse requests for personal information.
- Respond assertively if you are ever in an uncomfortable position online. Exit the program, turn off the computer, tell a trusted friend, or call the police.
- Report any suspicious or dangerous contact that makes you feel uncomfortable.

I-SAFE also advises young people to take these precautions:

- Protect your identifying information (name, sex, age, address, school, teams). It only takes a little information for a predator to identify you.
- Create a username and online profile that is generic and anonymous.
- Know how to exit an inappropriate website.

- Guard your pictures. You never know who may be looking at them.
- Keep in mind that chatroom "friends" are not always whom they say they are.

It is also important to develop protocols for camper use of social networking sites, especially those that link them to your camp or their fellow campers. Once the policies are completed, let your campers and their parents know of your policies in writing. You may also wish to monitor sites for compliance or, better still, encourage self-monitoring and reporting by members of your online camp community. One camper who believes that's the best approach says, "Camp directors should know what's going on, but it shouldn't be their responsibility to address it. We should be given the chance to monitor ourselves and if that doesn't work, the site should be shut down." Last but not least, notify campers and their parents when campers have violated your policy and follow-through with consequences.

Educating Parents

Camps can play a particularly valuable role in educating parents about the threats posed by social networking sites, arming them with strategies to help keep their children safe. Wiredsafety.org offers some online safety guidelines for parents.

- Personal information stays personal.
- Make sure your child doesn't spend all of his or her time on the computer.
- Keep the computer in a family room, kitchen, or living room, not in your child's bedroom. Knowing you are watching, kids are less likely to put themselves in risky situations, and you can safely oversee what's going on.
- Learn enough about computers so you can enjoy them together with your kids.
- Watch your children when they're online and see where they go.
- Make sure that your children feel comfortable coming to you with questions.
- Keep kids out of chatrooms unless they are monitored.
- Discuss these rules, get your children to agree to adhere to them, and post them near the computer as a reminder.
- Help them find a balance between computing and other activities.
- Remember to monitor their compliance with these rules, especially when it comes to the amount of time your children spend on the computer.
- Get to know their "online friends" just as you get to know all of their other friends.
- Warn them that people may not be what they seem to be. Predators often pose as children to gain our children's trust.

Developing Protocols for Staff

Camps are also well advised to develop protocols for their staff, prohibiting, for example, any online exchange that would be considered a violation of existing personnel policies and the posting of any inappropriate information or photos that can be accessed by campers. You can also use these sites as screening tools when hiring counselors, much as other businesses are doing. Already, reports are surfacing of students being denied jobs by prospective employers who have viewed their personal pages.

Don Schroeder, an employment lawyer in the Boston office of Mintz Levin, says, "While you may not be able to keep people from doing what they want on the Internet, you can certainly take action if you don't like what you see," including dismissing, or not rehiring, any staff member found to be in violation of the policies you have created. He offers the following tips:

- Consistently and fairly apply employment policies in order to avoid the appearance of disparate treatment of employees.
- Instruct your staff that they are prohibited from posting obscene, defamatory, profane, or libelous information.
- Inform your staff that they cannot disseminate any information about the camp that could be considered private, personal, or confidential, including but not limited to pictures of the camp site. Explain the consequences for violation of these policies (e.g., that they could be subjected to disciplinary action up to and including termination of employment).

Risks and Rewards

As with most things Internet, social networking sites offer content both bad and good. At worst, they perpetuate bawdy exhibitionism. At best, they provide a place for the meaningful exchange of creative ideas, memories, and dialogue, keeping young people connected to the friends and experiences that matter most. In that way, your space is their space, too.

19

Getting What You're Paying For

by Michael Weeks, P.E.

There are few things more frustrating for a consulting engineer than to have an owner spend money needlessly. Unfortunately, we do a miserable job educating clients about what we can do to help save them money and time in the long run. This month, we're going to try to change that by using another real-world project to illustrate how being penny wise can lead to a pound of foolishness.

Often, we go through years of planning, design, and permitting, and then, in the owner's rush to get the project under way, making certain that the product matches the plan is forgotten. The excitement of your project coming to life and the "keep things moving during construction mentality" causes many owners to make or accept major changes to the original design without understanding what the effects could be. An unsupervised contractor (or even a supervised one) may not be following the approved plans and details that you have hired him to build. Unless you can read construction drawings, how will you know that you're getting what you are paying for?

A Real-World Project

Some time ago, we completed the design and permitting of a roadway construction project. It involved setting the roadway geometry, pavement components, grading, sedimentation and erosion control, and storm-water management. Our contract with the owner ended with the township's approval, since he didn't want to pay us to help him choose a contractor or to check the work as it progressed. "After all," he reasoned, "the township is requiring that the contractor provide as-built drawings, so they'll have to do it right." When we delivered all of the permits and plans required to bid and build the project, he paid his bill and left and we heard nothing from him or about the project for almost a year. In his opinion, how hard could it be to build a 24-foot wide strip of pavement with 4-foot shoulders on either side? As construction moved along, the contractor made some "minor changes." When the owner was nearing the end of the project, he asked us to visit the site and check the contractor's "as-built" drawings. As it turned out, the changes hadn't been minor at all, and apparently construction was much more complicated than he had thought.

On my first site visit, I saw immediately that the road had been constructed without shoulders. Just beyond the edge of the pavement, the drainage ditch dropped off several feet. Without shoulders, there would be no place to stack plowed snow or to have a car parked with traffic getting by. I looked at the plans. I looked at the road. Clearly, this wasn't right, and this was just the first of a number of issues that were plainly incorrect.

As I drove through the "completed" project, it became clear that the high spots in the road were too high and the low spots were too low. Normally, roads are built using special survey stakes set at 25-foot intervals along the project that show the contractor how high the dirt and stone and asphalt should be. This ensures that the roads are not too steep, there are no blind spots for drivers, and that everything drains properly. In our case, it turns out that our owner had selected a contractor who believed that he was good enough to do without those guides and so had built the project "by eye." In addition, while he hadn't done a very good job building by eye, it was easy to see how wrong it was. Road slopes were eroding, sending runoff and earth onto adjacent property. One culvert was set so low that the road would flood. The incorrect vertical grade was caused by the contractor trying to avoid moving dirt and by grading without stakes, which completely changed the road profile from the design. While it made it much easier to construct, we ended up with an unsafe and unstable final product, which was encroaching on the neighbor's property. I wondered why the owner had me do a design at all.

I returned to the office and prepared a letter for the owner listing all of the deficiencies that I could see. Although the contractor at this point seemed very agreeable to resolving these issues and correcting the road, it took four more tries, four more reviews and deficiency letters, and two months to finally correct the problems.

Here's a hypothetical question: Do you think that a site-excavation contractor, who has been in business for 20 years or more can read a tape measure? Would you trust him to build according to the plan that you paid for? While this may over simplify the issue, our contractor was told, and was shown four times, that the roadway width was not in accordance with the plan. Each time he acknowledged this and agreed to make it right. Talk about déjà vu, every time I went to the site it still wasn't correct.

Many of these deficiencies may have very well been our (dumb, like a fox) contractor trying to cut corners that would have otherwise saved him a significant sum of money. However he had agreed to a contracted price based on the plans, and certainly he was not offering the owner a credit for these changes. In fact, the lawsuits that would have come from the adjoining property owner would probably have cost far more than the contractor was paid for the whole job.

In the end, our owner received a project that generally conformed to the plans as had been agreed. Although our contractor appeared incompetent at times, we were fortunate that he stayed on site to rectify the situation. (Often times, contractors will get angry and abandon the site, holding the owner hostage.) This could be attributed to two things—either morally and ethically the contractor felt obligated to provide the owner the contracted product, or the owner was smart and had yet to pay for the completed work.

What Did We Learn?

Although my example is specific to a new road project, it can be easily translated to any project, small or large, that you have going on at camp. Let's review some of the things that our owner did both right and wrong that could have drastically changed the outcome.

- What if our owner had been willing to authorize the additional expense of periodic construction observation? A single site review, weekly, comprising of a couple of hours by his design professional could have identified these problems before work had to be undone and redone, saving our owner the delays at the end of the job, as well as reducing the waste of the contractor's time and materials.

- What if our owner hadn't asked the design professional to complete a final review of the finished product? Without this review, he would not have known that the road slopes were extending onto the neighboring property (before the neighbor's lawyer filed suit) or that the stream would flood the road (before it washed out).

- What if our owner had paid the contractor the majority of the contract amount, because "It looks like it's done."? The owner probably would have never seen the contractor again, and the owner would have been left with an incomplete project and out a bunch of money.

- What if our owner had done some additional research on the contractor he hired? Was this just a freak occurrence by one particular contractor or a pattern? If the owner had not worked with this contractor before, he should have insisted on the contractor securing bonds to be certain that the project would be completed on time and in accordance with the plans. (For refresher information on what bonds do or how they work, read the Building Principles column, "Construction Contracting," in the May/June 2002 *Camping Magazine*.)

How Does This Apply to Camp?

Maybe you're thinking, "So what? What does all of this have to do with me and my camp?" Let's put it all into a camp context. What if this was your project that you brought back to us for review on June 1, just before camp opens? Could you afford to stop all traffic at the entrance to camp until August 1 because the road isn't built according to the plan?

There are several morals of this story that you can take to the bank for camp:

- By engaging an engineer to prepare a design, you are purchasing knowledge and skill of how all the project pieces work together.

- By keeping your engineer on the job to monitor construction on your behalf, you can rest easier knowing that your contractor is building what you're paying to have built.

- With regular checks during construction, you will have the benefit of being better able to gage how far the contractor has progressed, how much he should be paid along the way, and whether the project is on schedule.

With all of the other responsibilities you manage preparing for, during, and after camp, why not let the folks who prepared the design help ensure that you get the project that goes with the design you paid for?

20

Tips for Running a Better Summer Camp Business

by Dan Zenkel

Running a summer camp is a noble endeavor. Summer camps impart skills and values to all types of children. Nevertheless, every summer camp, small or large, private, religious, nonprofit or for-profit, is a business. If a summer camp takes in less money than it spends, it will eventually fail. Not coincidentally, summer camps that run well as businesses are usually effective in executing their mission. The same talents and skills required to run a business—focus, persistence, attention, and intelligence—are also required to run a quality summer program.

We have devoted much of the past eight years seeking to learn how to best manage summer camps. We certainly do not have all or even most of the answers. However, we do have some ideas and suggestions. This article compiles many of the ideas and tips that we have developed ourselves and adopted from veteran camp professionals.

The tips are organized into four categories: Revenue, Operating Expenses, Facility Management, and Miscellaneous. Not every idea or suggestion applies to every camp. Some apply only to traditional camps—those that occupy real estate, the primary purpose of which is for use as a summer camp. Other suggestions apply to nontraditional camps, which occupy real estate used primarily for noncamp purposes such as schools, churches, and community centers.

Revenue

"Revenue" is the money collected from all sources, tuition, vendor rebates, canteen charges, interest income, and, in the case of many nonprofits, donations and grants.

Since personnel related expenses account for more than half of most camp's expenses, and since such costs usually increase over time, camp revenues must also increase over time in order for the camp to survive and thrive. Here are some ways to increase your camp's revenue.

Tip 1—Measure and analyze your enrollment and your revenue.

Track your enrollment monthly and file your reports. Compare the current and prior year's enrollment at that time.

Each year, calculate and analyze your camp's re-enrollment percentage. Determine the number of campers eligible to return by taking the prior year's enrollment and subtracting the number of campers who are ineligible to return because of age. Then divide the number of returning campers by the number of campers eligible to return. A camp that runs seven weeks or more should aim for an 88 percent re-enrollment rate. Anything less than 80 percent is unacceptable. Camps with shorter sessions tend to have lower re-enrollment rates. A good target for a three- to four-week camp is 80 percent, and 60 percent is a good target for a two-week camp. Day camps that serve campers under 10 or 11 should aim for 65 percent re-enrollment. Those that serve campers up to 15 years of age should aim for 70 percent.

These industry standards are helpful, but the most important gauge is your own camp's historical performance. If your re-enrollment rate is improving, so is your camp, and you are headed in the right direction. Camps that run sessions of varying lengths should also track enrollment by the number of camper weeks.

Tip 2—If you're everything to everybody, you're nothing to anybody.

Like it or not, your camp is a brand. It means something to consumers—perhaps many, maybe only a few. Just as top brands like Wal-Mart® "Always Low Prices"; Bank of America "Higher Standards"; and Burger King® "Have It Your Way®" stand for something unique, so should your camp. Most of today's camps do not stand for anything unique. Scores of camps tout common catch-phrases like "Friendships for a Lifetime," or "Building Great Memories." Compare these to phrases such as "A Day Camp as Complete as Sleep Away," which is used by Camp Ramaquois in Rockland County, New York. Hearing this, a consumer immediately understands that her child will sleep at home yet have a sleep away like experience.

Hanging your hat on a unique positioning does not mean your camp cannot have other attributes. Indeed, depending on the type of camp you run, your camp must meet many qualifications. However, the quality camps in any given sector of the market, whether private sports camps, nonprofit religious camps, or special-needs camps, typically share many of the same attributes. These attributes are not differentiators. Rather, they are costs of entry—prerequisites to being considered as part of the category. For example, simply to be considered as one of the category of premium, full-season boys' sports camps, a camp must offer quality sports instruction; excellent, well-maintained facilities; and an organized and supervised program. All premium boys' camps share these attributes. The differentiating factors are often intangible and emotional. The chart below provides some examples of differentiators and costs of entry.

Differentiators vs. Cost of Entry	
Intangibles	
Values	Spirit
Traditions	Heritage
Camp Management/Cost of Entry	
Facilities	State-of-the-art equipment
Cleanliness	Organization and supervision
Safety	

Tip 3—Discover your brand positioning.

Understanding the need to discover your positioning is only the beginning. The next step, actually identifying that positioning, is much more difficult. There is no surefire path, but there are steps to help you find your way. Study your competitors. Gather their marketing materials and find out if they have staked out a position. Ask your parents and campers what makes your camp unique. Common themes will likely emerge. Latch onto those themes. Next, record various iterations of those themes and present them to your existing campers and camp families. Determine which ones they find appealing. Remember, you are not trying to be something you are not. You are trying to find the most appealing way to present what you are.

Here are some questions to ask your campers and camp parents to help you discover your positioning:

- What do you like best about Camp X?
- If you had the opportunity to tell our directors anything, what would it be?
- In your view, what makes Camp X, Camp X?

Provide parents and campers an open-ended opportunity to respond. Listen to the answers. Do not merely seek an affirmation.

Tip 4—Live your positioning and shout it to the world.

Once you settle on a positioning, you must share it with the world. If you do not constantly tell people what you stand for, then others, often your competitors, sometimes well-meaning outsiders, will fill the void. Their messages will certainly differ from yours. Include your positioning in every communication with your existing parents, campers, and those who express interest in your camp. Highlight it in all of your promotional materials, on your website, in your end-of-summer letter, in your prospect letter, in your ongoing newsletters and on your logoed camp clothing.

Tip 5—Every contact and communication is a marketing opportunity.

All contact between your camp and your current customers and prospects sends a message. Pay attention to how everything you do communicates your message. The chart below explains some of the subtle, sometimes unintended, signals conveyed during a tour given by a resident camp for prospective camp families.

Everything Provides A Signal
Empty field > Children don't do enough
Mess and garbage > Camp isn't safe
Children take a long walk to get from one point to another > Camp isn't structured
No central gathering place > Camp has no spirit

Operating Expenses

There are two types of expenses, operating and capital. The use of funds to provide services during the current year are termed operating expenses. Expenditures on projects lasting more than one year are capital expenditures. Salaries are operating expenses. The cost of a new building is a capital expenditure. Although the distinction between operating and capital expenditures is sometimes subtle, for purposes of this discussion, we assume the distinctions are clear. Controlling your operating expenses is just as important as increasing your revenue. The old Ben Franklin adage, "A penny saved is a penny earned," applies to every business.

Tip 6—Understand where to save.

People are the lifeblood of your camp and, indeed, of any business. Do not save money at the expense of keeping and rewarding good people. Rather, focus on saving money in other spending areas. Use the savings to retain and motivate your best people.

Tip 7—Track and analyze your spending.

The best and easiest way to control your expenses is to pay attention to them. The first step is to keep track by using accounting software. The Quickbooks® accounting software is inexpensive and easy to use. Use Quickbooks® or some other accounting software to set up your chart of accounts, which is a list of revenue and expense categories. Invoices, checks, and other spending records should be filed and easily accessible.

After setting up your chart of accounts, code every invoice, payroll charge, credit-card charge, and expense report to the correct account and file the backup. All accounting systems enable you to compare current and prior year spending in all of the accounts. Take advantage of this functionality. If you notice a steep increase in spending in a particular account, investigate until you understand. For example, if you notice a sharp rise in your spending on athletic supplies, create a report showing every athletic supply purchase for the current and prior year grouped by vendor. Review the larger invoices. Check your inventory of athletic supplies. How much inventory remains? Did you over order? Who is ordering? Are they ordering better or more expensive products than you need? Are two people ordering the same things? Eventually, the truth will emerge.

Tip 8—Pay attention to price.

Pay attention to the prices you pay. Long-distance telephone charges have fallen precipitously in recent years. Several years ago, these charges averaged seven cents a minute. Now they average less than four. If you are still paying seven, call your long-distance provider and pleasantly, but firmly request a reduction. If you don't get what you ask for, find a carrier who will charge less and switch to that carrier. Take a similar approach to cell phone charges. Check your monthly bill. If you are paying for minutes beyond your plan limit, contact your carrier and ask to change to a better plan. Shop around for your propane. Most summer camps pay too much for propane. One of the first things we do after purchasing a camp is compare the price that the camp pays for propane with the price that our other camps pay. Inevitably, the new camp is paying much more than our existing camps. We call the current supplier, explain that we understand that the price is too high, and kindly request a price reduction. The result is almost always an immediate 25-35 percent price reduction.

Tip 9—Bid where possible.

Most catalog vendors will provide price quotes. Indeed, many vendor catalogs invite camps to "contact us for a price quote." A new website developed by American Camp Association, New York, www.campshoppingnetwork.com, allows ACA members to simultaneously request via email multiple price quotes from vendors in a particular product category. Bid pricing generally beats the standard 10-percent discount that catalog vendors offer. If you do not have the time or inclination to prepare your own bids, you can engage an outside consultant to prepare and disseminate bids for you.

Tip 10—Special situation: camp laundry

If your camp has excess septic capacity or is connected to a public sewer line, then build your own laundry facility. In 2005, one of our camps spent $35,000 to convert a building into a working laundry and staffed it with six seasonal employees. The camp's laundry expense declined from $40,000 in 2004 to $15,000 in 2005. Another one of our camps built its own laundry and realized similar savings.

Tip 11—Special situation: abatement of real estate taxes

Challenge your real estate tax assessment at least every other year. Many attorneys will perform this service for a contingency fee and take one-third of any savings as compensation.

Tip 12—Special situation: food

Although food is generally the second largest expense at resident camps (after personnel), it is the least understood by camp directors. There are two, interrelated aspects of food cost: material and preparation. Generally, the better the chef, the lower the food cost. A more expensive chef can save you money. The following example is illustrative.

Analysis of Food Spending			
Category Description	Camp 1	Camp 2	Camp 3
Food	$145,000	$165,000	$165,000
Third-Part Food – (e.g., outside pizza)	$5,000	$10,000	$5,000
Total	$150,000	$175,000	$170,000
Chefs & Assistants	$60,000	$50,000	$60,000
Management (e.g., Sodexho)	$0	$0	$20,000
Total	$210,000	$225,000	$250,000

Camp 1 has an excellent chef and does not use a food service. It spent $200,000 on food. Camp 2's chef is not as accomplished. It spends less on personnel but more on food. Camp 3 uses a food service. While using a food service is convenient, it is also expensive.

This type of multi-account analysis applies to many spending categories. Personnel expenses are another example. Recruiting expense, salaries, foreign-staff fees and staff-travel expense, benefits, and payroll taxes and charges must be analyzed together to determine and understand personnel costs.

Facility Management Maintenance

Tip 13—Maintenance saves capital expenditures.

Over the long term, investment in basic infrastructure and maintenance, roofs, foundations, septic systems, paint and drainage, saves money by forestalling expensive capital projects. Water-tight roofs preserve buildings. Proper drainage prevents washouts that destroy buildings and roads. Maintaining septic systems avoids replacement and the costly, mandated upgrades attendant thereto. Keeping buildings off of the ground limits dry rot that undermines buildings.

Tip 14—Inspect and trim trees.

Falling trees and limbs are a significant hazard to people and buildings. Rarely and tragically, falling trees kill or seriously injure people at camp. Frequently, falling trees destroy valuable buildings. Dead or diseased trees and limbs should be removed and overhanging limbs should be trimmed away from roofs and pedestrian paths. Trees with roots growing under paved surfaces such as a court or road should also be removed. At least once every five years, retain a certified arborist to mark all hazardous trees in the immediate vicinity of buildings or people. Remove the hazardous trees. Cutting back trees has the added benefit of enhancing views.

Tip 15—Adopt and enforce a zero tolerance graffiti policy.

Graffiti, which usually appears on cabin, cubby, and bathroom walls, should not be tolerated. It is an eyesore, and its presence sends an unwanted message—that the camp takes little pride in its appearance and cannot control its campers. The only way to prevent graffiti or to rid a camp of graffiti is to remove all of it, by paneling or painting (sanding won't work), and then adopting and strictly enforcing a zero tolerance policy. All staff must be enlisted in the effort. As soon as graffiti is spotted, it must be removed by the offender. A two-time offender should be sent home.

Some camps contend that their graffiti appeals to returning alumni who search the cabins for their names. Graffiti's negative impacts far outweigh this benefit. Bunk plaques are an excellent alternative. Every session, each cabin group creates a plaque listing its campers and counselors. The plaques, which are displayed in each cabin, enhance the cabin's appearance and confirm the camp's commitment to tradition and continuity.

Tip 16—Consider a trash compactor.

Camps that have multiple garbage dumpsters on site should consider installing a trash compactor. Dumpsters, which attract bears and other animals, can create an unsightly mess. Many waste collection companies will lease a compactor to a camp. The camp's only upfront expenses are the cost of bringing electricity to the site and of pouring a concrete pad. The annual costs of using dumpsters or a compactor are approximately equal; however, the compactor offers enormous maintenance benefits. It does not attract bears, reduces the number and duration of waste pickups, and neatens up the camp.

Tip 17—New fences make a big difference.

A cost-effective method of improving a camp's aesthetics is to remove old, chicken-wire fencing or netting that serves as fencing and replace it with black, chain-link fencing. The expense can be limited by retaining and painting the existing fence posts and attaching the new fencing to those posts.

Tip 18—Good maintenance staff need little direction.

If you find it necessary to continually provide your maintenance director with a list of projects, replace him. A good maintenance director proactively and continuously makes and updates his own lists of projects. This is not to say that a director who walks the camp property and makes notes is wasting her time. Two or three sets of eyes are always better than one. However, a good maintenance staff fixes most problems before the director notices.

Tip 19—Clean up your environmental messes.

Having a dumpsite at your camp is convenient, but when it comes time to borrow or sell, it will be a headache. If you have an old dump, clean it up. If you can't afford to clean it all at once, clean a little at a time. Likewise, remove all underground gas and oil tanks and replace them with above-ground tanks that have secondary containment. Underground tanks can leak without your knowledge. Spills are expensive and time consuming to remediate. If you remove a tank or a dump, retain a licensed contractor or professional consultant to assist you. This will spare you further expense by insuring that the remediation is properly documented.

Tip 20—Beware of "grandfathered" septic systems.

Many camp owners contend that they can continue to use a septic system that does not meet current health codes because the system's construction predates those codes and is therefore "grandfathered," i.e. permitted to continue in use even though it does not comply with current codes. True, a functioning septic system that predates the current septic code is generally grandfathered. However, most septic systems eventually fail. When they do, they must be replaced with code compliant systems. Take an inventory of your "grandfathered" systems and gradually replace those that do not comply with current codes.

Capital Expenditures

Tip 21—Reinvest in your facility.

Failure to consistently reinvest in facility upkeep will eventually catch up to any camp. The camp will garner a reputation as "run down" and will find it increasingly difficult to attract new campers.

Tip 22—Showpiece buildings feed the ego but may not feed your family.

Many summer-camp owners take great pride in their facilities. They consider their camps as extensions of themselves, expression of their identity. Some build breathtaking buildings. The construction of such buildings, although personally satisfying, doesn't always makes good business sense. Few people choose a camp based on its impressive buildings. Current and prospective camp families want to see that buildings are neat, clean, and in good repair. Most do not care if the camp has the "nicest buildings." The exception is a camp that positions itself as the "best that money can buy," or simply, "the best." Since it is difficult for any camp to prove that it has the best programming or the best staff, the one area where a camp can objectively support its claim to being the best is in the size and scope of its buildings. These reinforce a "best camp" positioning and are a wise choice for a camp seeking to capture that market.

Tip 23—Neatness counts.

Keep your camp neat and clean. A messy camp sends a message about camp safety. A visitor asks herself, consciously or unconsciously, "If the camp's directors tolerate this mess, how do I know they are making sure my child is safe?"

Tip 24—Signs matter.

Signs enhance a camp's appearance by tying the camp together in a visually appealing way. They also enhance a camp's brand by consistently displaying the camp's name and logo. Signs also help new campers, staff, parents, and visitors navigate the camp. Finally, consistent signage conveys the message that camp is well-organized.

Miscellaneous

Tip 25—Get along with the local community.

Camps that take their neighbors for granted do so at their peril. Irate neighbors can ruin a camp director's summer or her entire year. Unhappy neighbors are more likely to complain to the local authorities, question a camp's zoning, or complain to the police. Fortunately, it is usually (though not always) easy to maintain good relations with the neighbors and the community. The best way to keep your neighbors happy is to limit ambient noise, especially early in the morning and late at night. Do not invite post-camp groups that will disturb your neighbors. Face loudspeakers inwards, away from the neighbors. Contribute to local charities. Every contribution, however small, is appreciated. Join the local lake association. Invite the neighbors over for a picnic. Arrange for campers to perform in front of a community organization like a home for the elderly. Arrange for your campers to paint the local library. Send out a pre-camp letter announcing your camp dates and the dates of any particularly boisterous events such as a carnival or color war break.

Tip 26—Don't nickel and dime your customers.

Camp tuition represents a large expense for most people and a financial sacrifice for many. Don't stick your customers with petty charges (e.g., $30 for a photograph on visiting day or $5 for a video of a recital). Give them the photo or the video, or, if you can't afford that, don't do it at all.

Tip 27—Enhance your existing programs.

Great organizations focus on what they do best. Few try to satisfy everyone. Feel free to add new programs but not at the expense of your existing programs. If you add a program, seriously consider removing another program that is not up to par.

Tip 28—Be your own biggest critic; confront the brutal facts.

The only way to improve is to discover and understand your weaknesses. Take surveys. Talk to your campers and your camp families. Invite criticism. Criticism may be painful to hear, but it must be heard. One school of thought holds that "Sleeping dogs should be let lie." I disagree. The risk of stirring up criticism is far less than the risk of not addressing a problem because you don't know it exists.

Tip 29/30—Admit your mistakes and apologize for them.

If you make a mistake, admit it, apologize, and explain how you will correct the mistake or prevent a recurrence. Two examples follow:

1. Your camp generates noise late at night that disturbs your neighbors. Send your neighbors a letter apologizing and explaining what you will do to prevent a recurrence. Then, follow up to make sure that you do not repeat your mistake.

2. You neglect to follow through on a promise to a parent, and the parent inquires about the promise. Apologize to the parent and explain what you will do to make sure the promise is kept. Then follow up to make sure the request is satisfied, and call the parent to tell them so. Humans have a great capacity for forgiveness. They have no capacity for being ignored.

About the American Camp Association

The American Camp Association (ACA) is a community of camp professionals dedicated to ensuring the high quality of camp programs, a greater public understanding of and support for the value of the camp experience, and an increase in the number of children, youth, and adults of all social, cultural, and economic groups who participate in the camp experience. Established in 1910, ACA operates as a private, nonprofit educational organization with members in all 50 states and several foreign countries. Its members represent a diverse constituency of camp owners and directors, executives, educators, clergy, businesses, consultants, camp and organization staff members, volunteers, students, retirees, and other individuals associated with the operation of camps for children and adults.